A GLIMPSE OF
OLD PEAKS ISLAND

THROUGH ROSE-COLORED GLASSES

A GLIMPSE OF
OLD PEAKS ISLAND

THROUGH ROSE-COLORED GLASSES

Reta Morrill *Alice Boyce*

Eunice Curran

Ellin Gallant *Joyce O'Brien*

Alice Boyce
Eunice Curran
Ellin Gallant
Reta Morrill
Joyce O'Brien

Library of Congress Control Number: 2009911538
ISBN: Hardcover   978-1-4415-8846-3
                   Softcover   978-1-4415-8845-6

This book was printed in the United States of America.

Book Cover by Jacqueline Gallant Bruns
All of the photographs in the book are from the authors' personal collections.

To order additional copies of this book, contact:
Xlibris Corporation
1-888-795-4274
www.Xlibris.com
Orders@Xlibris.com
67405

Contents

Dedication

This Book is dedicated to our parents who brought us up in very difficult times but always made us feel safe, secure and loved.

ACKNOWLEDGEMENTS

THANK YOU TO our family and friends for their help, encouragement, and patience throughout the several years it has taken to make this book a reality. We also want to thank Benita Fugelso for allowing us to use excerpts from her mother's book *Experiences of My Early Life on House Island* by Roberta Randall Sheaff.

In addition, thanks to Deborah Lyons for editing the book and Bailey O'Brien and Chelsea Vergers for their help and expertise with the pictures.

INTRODUCTION

THE INSPIRATION FOR this book occurred on a beautiful Fall day in September, 1989 when the Peaks Island Grammar School and Community Reunion of the 1920's, 1930's and 1940's was held at Greenwood Garden. It was a true "family reunion". Graduates and former residents came from all over the country.

There are so few of us left who remember Peaks Island before the war that the five of us, Alice, Ellin, Eunice, Joyce and Reta decided to write this book. After many long lunches, lots of laughs and tears we settled down and got serious.

CHAPTER ONE

HISTORY

OUR BOOK BEGINS by exploring some of the important events and notable people of past years.

Many books have been written about the early settlers, one of these, *A History of Peaks Island and Its People*, written in 1897 by Nathan Goold, a Maine historian, begins in 1623 when Christopher Levitt sailed into Casco Bay. The following is an excerpt from the book:

> "It is fitting that the story of their lives should be preserved, that those who come after them may know who they were and what were the events in their lives that went to make up the history of the island while they lived. They were a settlement

by themselves and shared each other's joys and sorrows. They saw the sun rise from out of the sea and the ocean was their highway".

In 1636, Sir Ferdinando Gorges, founder of the Province of Maine, gave George Cleeves a commission for all of the land and islands between Cape Elizabeth and Sagadahoc River and up into the mainland 60 miles. Some years later, George Cleeves' descendents married Bracketts and settled on Peaks Island. The first families suffered many hardships and the island was not resettled again until the 1700's.

The island, comprising something over 700 acres, was nearly equally divided into three farms, owned and occupied by three men and their families. Thomas Brackett owned the southerly end running from Jones Landing and Greenwood Garden to the farther shore. Joshua Trott, married to a Brackett, owned the central portion of the island extending northbound to the vicinity of Brackett Church and, as Mr. Brackett, from shore to shore. The northerly end, including Trefethen and Evergreen, was owned by Colonel John Waite and later purchased by Henry Trefethen in 1843.

At the beginning of the 1800's there were only a few families living on the island. One of these was Henry Mansfield Brackett born in 1812 and an heir to the Brackett estate. He married Sarah Hadlock from the Cranberry Islands and built a house in the Hadlock Cove area called "Summer Retreat". It was the first boarding house on the island and had picnic grounds and a bowling alley.

Henry also built a wharf. A newsletter "The Islander" dated November 12, 1937 describes the beginning of steamboat service in Casco Bay. The article stated that they first ran in 1822 and in later years one of the steamboats operated between Portland and Brackett Cove in Whitehead Passage. Henry died in 1879 at age 59; his widow later married Dr. Torrington and they made their home at Summer Retreat.

Mr. Brackett was very influential in the community. He and Mr. Trefethen were behind the drive to build the Brackett Memorial Church and also the present school. The Brackett family cemetery is located at the southwest point west of Torrington Beach. Wesley Scott, Henry and Sarah's adopted son served in the Civil War in the 1st Marine Calvary Regiment and was captured and died in Salisbury prison at the age of 19 years, 6 months, and 22 days according to the monument erected in his memory in the family cemetery. The homestead still stands and is now a private residence. Reta remembers her dad driving guests from the boat to stay there.

William Jones was another man held in high regard A reference to him in Goold's book tells of him being orphaned at age 12 and at 14 walking from Portsmouth, New Hampshire to Boston, Massachusetts, looking for employment. He met up with Capt. John Brackett in a tavern where he was working and sailed to Portland on Capt. Brackett's ship. He became a cooper (a maker of barrels and tubs), working in different locations eventually coming to Peaks where he established a cooper shop. He built the Union House, the largest of the boarding houses at that time. Jones Landing is named for him. A house on the site was moved from down front to the warmer southwest side and is located at the corner of

Whitehead Street and Seashore Avenue. Before being moved, one of the rooms in the house was used as the island post office and the slots for mail still are there.

Jones Landing

Benjamin Welch Jr. and his brother George both married into the Brackett family in the early 1800's and became owners of a portion of the Brackett estate. Benjamin Junior was born in 1828 and left Peaks Island at an early age and ended up in Sacramento California, as a superintendent of the Car Building Works of the Union Pacific Railroad. In 1865 he conducted the first immense snowplow used by the Central Pacific Railroad Company, In 1869 he invented a framer and tenon machine which proved to be a great time and labor saver in car construction. In 1870, on his plans, the first immigrant sleeper car was built, afterwards known as the tourist car, a device that was adopted by most railroad companies in the United States.

He remained in California but visited Peaks Island occasionally. The following is an excerpt from a Sacramento newspaper clipping dated March 29, 1906:

> "It seems that there has been in the possession of the Welch Family a track of land on Peaks Island in Casco Bay just three miles from the city of Portland, Maine. The island is one of the loveliest upon the continent and a great resort. Over two years ago, the Welch Company, of which Uncle Ben is the head, erected on the island a beautiful summer hotel."

In another clipping, referring to one of his visits:

> "A family reunion was held at the Old Homestead. Among those present were the Benjamin Welch family, his sister, Mary Adams, Dr. Torrington and his wife, the widow of Henry M. Brackett, Esq. in whose family Benjamin had lived for several years when a boy. After dinner several hours were pleasantly spent in social conversation about the days of Old Lang Syne and the party broke up perhaps never to meet again this side of the river."

On Monhegan Island, in 1826, Henry Trefethen built the house called "The Influence", which is now in the national historic register and is privately owned. His father had purchased Monhegan in 1797; however, there is no record that he ever lived there. Henry's son, also Henry, moved from Monhegan to House Island in 1823 and shared a house with his cousin John Starling (or Sterling). Henry and wife Mary (called Polly) celebrated their fiftieth wedding anniversary on House Island. On Sundays she dressed in black silk, to be rowed over to Peaks Island to church services. Earlier services were held on House Island before 1860 when the Methodist Church was built. Both Henry and Polly died in 1880 and are buried in Pond Grove Cemetery.

The Influence

In 1843 Henry bought two-ninths of Peaks Island from the Waite heirs, from the back shore to the bay. He had "The Homestead", a double house, built at the corner of Trefethen and Pleasant Avenues for his two oldest children. His son, William S. (Reta's great, great, grandfather) gave the City of Portland 7 acres of land for roads which were given family names: Trefethen Avenue, Prince Avenue, Reed Avenue and Skillings Road. The plot of land that is Reed Park was given in memory of his wife, Emily Brackett Reed.

The Homestead

William S. or Captain Trefethen, as he was known, together with William Jones (owner of the Union House and Jones Landing) were responsible for the grading and widening of Island Avenue; changing it from a path for cows, oxen and foot traffic to a more usable road. Capt. Trefethen also planted elm trees to border Island Avenue. The Trefethens built Trefethens Landing and William S. built "The Montreal House", a hotel, later renamed "The Valley View House" located where the tennis courts are now. The hotel became very popular, especially with Canadians. The hotel was surrounded by a fruit orchard according to Jessie Trefethen in her book, *Trefethen, The Family and the Landing*. It must have been lovely when the fruit trees were in bloom. The Valley View House was sold after Captain Trefethen's death in 1907 and it burned to the ground the following year. Reta' s grandmother remembered when "Trefethen, Maine" was a valid post office address and the post office was in Webber's store. Her grandmother also remembered going for rides with her grandfather, Capt. Trefethen, in his horse and buggy with the fringed top. Capt. Trefethen was the first islander to have a horse and his barn/stable became Webbers store.

VALLEY VIEW HOUSE, TREFETHEN, ME., LOOKING TOWARD PORTLAND HARBOR.
Published by Mrs. S. F. Heath.

Valley View House

Valley View House at Trefethen Landing

Capt. Trefethen's stable

From Box 37
Trefethen Me.

PIONEER FAMILIES REUNION
PEAKS ISLAND, MAINE
71694

Trefethen, Maine Postmark

Thomas Brackett Reed was elected to Congress representing the first Maine district and served from 1876 to 1899. His father, grandfather and his great grandfather were all born on the island.

Thomas Brackett Reed

Reed was known for his large physique (6'3" and 275" pounds), wit and brilliant parliamentary skill. He was mentioned for the Republican nomination for President in 1892 and 1896. When asked about his chances for receiving the nomination he answered, "They could do worse and they probably will." In his first term as Speaker of the House, he earned the nickname "Czar". He forced Congress to adopt "Reed's Rules" of procedure, which made the silent quorum impossible. This tactic had been used to paralyze legislation. Congressman not answering were not counted as a quorum, even if they were in their seats. When Reed counted the silent Democrats present, pandemonium resulted. Reed stood firm, requesting "those members who say they are not present to be seated".

He could be sarcastic. Once a congressman said he would rather be right than be president. Reed responded, "Don't worry, you'll never be either." Reed opposed the Spanish-American War and the annexation of Hawaii and the Philippines. In 1899 when he decided to end his congressional career and resign, he wrote his Maine constituents: "Whatever may happen, I am sure the 1ST Maine District will always be true to the principles of liberty, self-government and the rights of man". A statue was erected in his honor on the Western Promenade.".

Towards the end of the 1800's what had been a very small community with only a few families and houses had now grown to a very popular summer colony. Greenwood Garden was the center of attraction with its opera house, merry-go-round, bandstand, its five story observatory and many other amusements. An advertisement showed "twenty-five cents round trip boat ride to Peaks Island which includes admission to the Opera House, choice seats extra." There were fireworks, daily balloon ascensions, concerts, wild animals, a magician and more.

Forest City Landing from the water

Down Front from the landing

Water view

Ferry at Forest City Landing

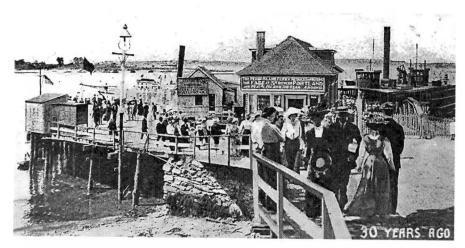

Forest City Landing

Gem Theater and Peaks Island House

Interior of Gem Theater

Peaks Island House

PEAKS ISLAND HOUSE, PEAKS ISLAND, ME.

Where Grandfather was born August 2nd, 1827

Peaks Island House

The Gem theater was built in 1888 and was first used as a skating rink and did not become a theater until 1898 when it was converted. It was a very odd-looking building, but very beautiful inside and seated many people. The island's popularity extended far and wide as there was overnight boat service from Boston and New York City to Portland. Picnickers came by the hundreds not just for the entertainment but to enjoy the beautiful island.

The first American summer stock was formed on Peaks in 1888 according to Nor' By East, an island newsletter. "A thespian, Bartley McCullum, was confronted with a problem. He had been signed to perform in a play scheduled for a fall run in New Jersey, but a summer of unemployment faced him. He persuaded the owner of the pavilion to lease it to him. He then staged a play called "Shaughram" with the cast of a New York theatrical company. The first night receipts totaled $2.05 but by the end of the week the theater was crowded. This was the beginning of summer stock. His company played the Peaks Island Theater for twelve years until it moved to a theater in Cape Elizabeth but summer stock continued at Peaks until World War I." Throughout its history, the Barrymores performed along with many other well-known actors of that era.

By this time the island had many hotels and boarding houses to accommodate the visitors. The Peaks Island House was built in the early 1800's and enlarged in later years as a boarding house. A second Peaks Island House, much larger, was built in 1903. Some of the others in the Forest City Landing area were the Bay View House, Union House, Coronado Hotel, Summer Retreat and the Innes House. The Civil War veterans of the Fifth and Eighth Maine Regiments each built a place to hold their annual gatherings.

Casco Bay became popular with yachtsmen, and large yachts were often anchored off Peaks Island. J. P. Morgan, the financier, and Cyrus H.K. Curtis, publisher, were visitors. Curtis was the donor of the Kotzschmar organ at City Hall.

Boat service to the island improved over the years as business grew. Eventually we had three landings, Forest City, Trefethen, and Evergreen Landings. This was very convenient for visitors and residents alike since most people walked.

TREFETHEN'S LANDING, PORTLAND HARBOR, MAINE.

Trefethen Landing

Trefethen Landing

Boat landing at Trefethen

The wharf at Trefethen

Evergreen Landing

Evergreen Landing

Peaks Island from Great Diamond Island

Several of the old homesteads on the island still remain, among these are five on Pleasant Avenue built by members of the same family, The Parsons. The first to arrive was Henry in 1804 from Gloucester MA.

Henry built the Parsons homestead in 1818 and later on his sons built the house beside it. Both of these houses have been extensively renovated in recent years but if one looks carefully the original architecture can be seen. The third Parsons' home is across the street from the homestead and was built by Henry's son, Samuel.

The oldest house on the island

Charles Parsons, another son of Henry's, built a house further up the road from his father's house. We remember Charles grand-daughter, Arlette Frellick living there when we were young. Across the street was the last Parsons house; it was built by Henry's grandson Edward for his daughter, Truelette, Arlette's sister (their sister, Charlette, lived in one of the other Parsons houses).

Arlette wrote a charming memoir to be presented to the Calends Club, a women' study group, for their 25th anniversary in 1953. In it she recalls being at Evergreen Landing in 1877-1878 when she was about ten. At that time, Evergreen Landing and the vicinity was the amusement center of Peaks Island. She remembered a dance hall, a restaurant and a bowling alley there. These were owned by members of the Sterling Family, originally of House Island, who owned all of Evergreen. At some point, it was gated probably near the corner of Trefethen and Island Avenues (hopefully the last gated community on the island). There were no cottages then; however, many people pitched tents on the Bay side. Later many of them built cottages on those sites.

Roads were now in place and businesses flourished. There was even talk about secession. On January 11, 1883 islanders met at Island Hall to discuss the feasibility of separation from the City of Portland. In 1901 there was an attempt made by a group of investors from Boston to build a scenic electric railway to circle the island. Fortunately it never materialized.

Water had been supplied by wells until 1906 when E. E. Rounds started the Peaks Island Water and Light Company. At first gas was used for power, then later electricity. Many of the older homes still have the original gas fixtures. The following is from a newspaper clipping dated June 17, 1924:

"The power plant at Peaks Island is fast nearing completion. The engines were given a stiff tryout the first of the week and were found to be working smoothly. It is expected that the lights will be turned on along the main streets the first of July."

In 1927 the Casco Bay Light and Power was formed on Island Avenue. It supplied not only Peaks, but other Casco Bay islands, and continued until 1965 when it was taken over by Central Maine Power Company.

Telephone service came in 1904, but it was only seasonal and in business locations until 1914 when it became year round. The office was closed in 1949 when the office was converted to dial service.

HOUSE ISLAND

Our neighboring island, House Island, played a part in the lives of our early settlers. Two of these, the Trefethen and Sterling (Starling) families moved from Monhegan Island to House Island in the early 1820's where they built and shared a house. They were in the dry fish (fish flakes) business and the granite piers still remain that were the docks for the fishing vessels.

Fish Houses

In later years an immigration station, hospital and doctor's house was built.

The following excerpts are from the book *Experiences of My Early Life on House Island on Casco Bay* by Roberta Randall Sheaff, whose father was an administrative engineer for the Public Health Service.

"When riding by House Island on one of the local ferries, or by Fort Scammel on one of the ships going to Nova Scotia, I am filled to overflowing with many memories; memories of a childhood never to be lived again, by anyone. House Island, in the harbor of Portland, Maine, is one of the advertised 365 islands in Casco Bay, about one-half mile long. Government-owned for many years, it is about three and one half miles from Portland and one half mile from Peaks Island."

"I was born on House Island, a quarantine station, in 1909 in one of the three houses there. My family, consisting of my father, mother and sister, who is five years older than I, and myself, were the only people living on the island, except for a few weeks in the summer when the Public Health Doctor from Portland and his family lived in the house on the hill, better known as the Doctor's house. The third building was a small hospital which had been used for smallpox patients. I cannot remember its ever being used while I lived there, because vaccination had pretty well eliminated that disease. Papa was in the United States Public Health Service as an administrative engineer assigned to the station."

"I remember the house in which we lived. It was a large gray clapboard frame house situated on the opposite point from Fort Scammel. It had a long hall running from one end to the other; and it was in a large room at one end of the hall that I was born. Some of the rooms were used for storage of government property. These rooms were seldom entered except at inventory time. We occupied most of the first floor and only one room on the second floor, which my sister and I shared in the summer. There were pot-bellied stoves in each room, although we never heated the bedrooms. The stoves provided us with adequate heat. We burned coal mostly, although a few sticks of wood would take off the chill during the cool days of spring and fall. Kerosene lamps lighted our home, wall fixtures in each room holding them. A large table lamp was always in the center of our dining room table. I remember the large globe-shaped lamp with the slender chimney showing through the opening in the top.

One might think this sounds like a lonely existence but I cannot recall our ever feeling lonely. We were all kept busy with varied activities. There were always chores to be done. As I remember it, Papa had to watch for the ships entering the harbor with a yellow flag flying. He would then notify the Quarantine office. The Public Health Doctor would have to board her and inspect her for sickness among the crew members. The American Flag had to be raised each morning and lowered each night at exactly sundown. Sometimes, when I helped my father, we had to be very careful when folding it because he would never let the flag touch the ground; that was disrespectful. Our fresh water had to be pulled up from the well daily. We had a cistern of rain water at the side of our house, with a pump in the kitchen, to supply us with water for washing purposes. Lamp chimneys had to be washed and the lamps filled with kerosene. The chickens, the cow and pig had to be fed and watered. In the summer the cow was put out to graze. The barn, where "Rhoda" the cow lived, was about a five minute walk from the house; and many evenings after the temperature had dropped, my father would walk to the barn to be sure Rhoda was warm enough. On the way back he would stop to check on the chickens. Sometimes Mama and Flora, my sister, and I would go with him. We sold our surplus milk to Brackett's store on Peak Island. The bottle caps were hand-stamped with "Grade A Milk – Fresh and Pure". Milk was not homogenized in those days, therefore the cream was inches thick at the top of the bottles, and customers in Brackett's store were usually waiting for "Randall's" milk. An annual inspection by a veterinary was necessary to give us permission to sell our "raw" milk, as pasteurization had become a requirement for regular dairies.

Papa always had a large garden which kept my mother busy canning vegetables. He cut enough hay in the summer to feed Rhoda during the winter. It was especially fun to ride on top of the hay in the hayrack as Papa pulled the rack to the barn. The island had to be watched constantly as tourists were allowed to land only at the Fort. I remember a huge sign at the entrance to the Fort end of the island that read "Cable Crossing – Do Not Anchor". During World War I the sign was removed because the Government did not want the enemy to know where our cable was located.

My sister and I helped Mama with the housekeeping as she was never very well. We shared some of the cooking duties. Pies were my specialty. Most of the laundry had to be ironed in those days. Mama always put on a clean housedress every afternoon, then wore that one the next morning to work in. Curtains were quite a job; they had to be starched, sprinkled and ironed and most of ours were ruffles! We were allowed to fish from the wharf but only from the railing. The wharf was within sight of our house so our mother could keep an eye on us at all times. There were strawberry patches down by the windmill, also chokecherries, raspberries, blueberries and blackberries to pick. It was fun to explore the many beach areas that were near enough for our parents to keep a watchful eye on us. On Sundays we seldom missed Sunday School on Peaks Island. Papa would row us over in his peapod, a double-ended boat similar to a dory and extremely sturdy. He kept it moored between two rock pilings with a pulley to the beach. A large motor boat was available to us but we didn't use it much as it was difficult to handle alone, especially in rough weather. The steps on the pier could be very slippery with the moss and seaweed left by the tide and my father didn't feel it was safe for us; so most of the time we used the peapod.

When my sister started school my father made two trips to Peaks every day. Later I joined them. Then when my sister went to high school in Portland and I was still in grammar school on Peaks, he had to make four round trips to Peaks every school day. Some of those trips were very rough. Some days we would be in grammar school, but children living on Peaks wouldn't have attended that day. The next day the teacher would ask why they were not in school and they would tell her that the weather was too stormy for them to go out. The teacher would tell them that if the Randall girls could get to school from House Island, there was no excuse for their not getting there. It just never occurred to us how difficult many of those trips must have been for Papa. On pleasant days, when the water was without a ripple, it would take less than ten minutes to row to Peaks; but other times it would take an hour or more.

Many days, I can remember, we would be already on Peaks when the "no school" alarm would ring; so we would turn around and go home. Before I was old enough to go to school I used to stand in the dining room window to watch my father row my sister to Peaks, especially on those stormy, windy days when the peapod would go out of sight between the huge white-capped waves. My mother didn't dare to watch. I was so excited to tell her and she would hold her breath until I said "Oh, there they are on top of the waves now". On warm evenings, after dinner, my father would often row us to Peaks for an ice cream cone or a bag of popcorn. What a long trip for a five cent ice cream!

The winters used to be more severe than in recent years. At times the ice would be so frozen, Papa would have to break it with one foot over the bow of the boat, then row the few inches he had broken away, and then start all over again. Other times it would spray over our "ulsters" which were heavy, heavy coats we wore over our school clothes to keep us warm and dry. All this time my father would be reminding us to stomp our feet and wave our arms so they wouldn't freeze. Quite an experience for a father whose daughters thought this was quite normal. It never occurred to us that we were having an unusual childhood. There were other times when the harbor was so frozen over that he couldn't possibly row any farther than where the tide made the freezing water slushy. So our father would row us out from the beach as far as he could. Then the old Swampscott, the ferry that ran from Portland to Peaks, would stop and Papa would boost us over the stern. The purser, Walter Crandall, would always be there to pull us onto the ferry; and in this way we would get to school.

We always had to take our lunch to school and eat in the classroom, while the other children went home. They used to think we were so lucky because we were having a picnic every day! Occasionally we would be invited to a friend's home for lunch. For us, that was a treat.

Every Monday was wash day. Two wash tubs were put on a standard with a hand wringer between them. My father did the scrubbings after my mother had boiled the clothes in a large tub that fit over two dampers on the coal and wood range in the kitchen. Watching the clothes dry on the lines, in the wide open spaces the island provided, is a decided change from the automatic driers that most of us use today.

One day the maid, at the Doctor's house on the hill, and I decided we would row to Peaks Island and spend some time. My mother, thinking I was visiting Mary, as I often did, was not concerned with my absence until a friend of hers on Peaks called her on the telephone to ask if she knew I was over there. My surprised mother asked her if she would tell us to come home immediately. By the time we started to row back the wind had come up, and was too strong for me, so I was slowly going out to sea. My father was watching and realized I was in difficulty so he started out for us. As the same time a passing motorboat stopped and gave us a tow. Needless to say I never did that again!

In winter there were the usual activities we enjoyed such as snowshoeing, skiing and sliding. Schoolwork took a great deal of our time in the evenings. On cold nights Mama would heat bricks on the kitchen range and then wrap them in a piece of blanket and put one in each of our beds so when we crawled inside the covers we would be nice and warm.

Living on an island we had to have a food supply adequate for several weeks. We always had two barrels of flour, one for bread and one for pastry. Our lard supply was in a large firkin. A hundred pounds of sugar was an ordinary purchase. Our cow and chickens kept us supplied with fresh eggs, milk and heavy cream. I can remember our slaughtered pig hanging in the outer hall all winter where it was very cold, our only means of refrigeration for such a large supply of meat. We kept smaller perishables in a pail lowered into the well where it was always cold.

I especially remember Christmastime. My father would cut down a large tree, on Peaks, which just filled an alcove by the door to the dining room. It was decorated a week before Christmas. On Christmas morning my sister and I were up long before daybreak; and, as we opened each gift, we would run down the long hall to our parents' bedroom to show them our surprises from Santa.

When my mother was in Portland for a day of shopping and my father didn't know on which trip she was returning, she would wave up to the Captain of the Swampscot, from the bow of the boat, as it was approaching House Island. He would blow his whistle 3 times, to alert my father and he would start for Peaks to pick her up. This was before we had a telephone. On many Sundays we would hear whistles blowing but we never knew who our company was until Papa returned from Peaks with them.

Even though I have observed my 50th wedding anniversary, the experiences on House Island are still very vivid in my mind and I realized it was a childhood not to be lived again, as our life-styles have been through so many changes since then!"

CHAPTER TWO

DOWN FRONT

W E GREW UP in the best of times in spite of the depression, a world war with atomic weapons and the Cold War that followed.

There were many descendents of the early settlers still living on the island: Brackett, Trott, Woodbury, Parson, Sterling, Jones, Skillings, Trefethen, Waite, and Welch families. They were hardy individuals who struggled through difficult times.

It was a close community. We knew each other by name and where we lived. We knew every house, cottage road and path. The whole island was our playground and the sea was our boundary.

Down Front, especially during the summer, was (as it is now) the hub of island activity and always busy, especially at boat-time. Lets stroll along the boardwalk which started at Greenwood Garden and continued onto Trefethen Landing.

Greenwood Garden, although it had passed its former glory was still a very inviting place. There were not as many trees; instead it was a beautiful grassy park-like area. A bandstand stood in the center of the green and popular bands came from town to entertain us. The old merry-go-round was still standing, but not operational. A few of the horses found homes on the island after it was dismantled. The playhouse hadn't been used for many years and wouldn't be again until aspiring actors came in the late 1930's or early 1940's.

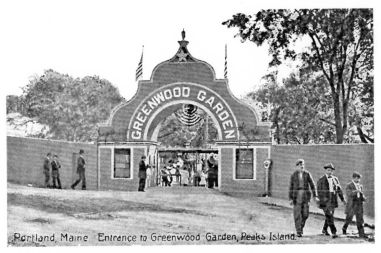

Entrance to Greenwood Garden

Next to the garden was the bowling alley. We had several bowling leagues, both men and women, island boys were pin boys. Each alley had a different tilt. If you bowled on alley number six, for example, you would start on the right hand side of the alley and bowl toward the left and with any luck it might end up in the center. This made bowling quite a challenge and bowling in town even more so. In later years under new management it stayed open all year but the sagging alleys never changed. There was a shooting gallery beside the bowling alley which is now a private residence. A front section opened up showing the moving clay duck targets. In later years the building became a bakery.

Charlie Brown's store was what is now the Peaks Island House. It is the original building and has had many renovations. Charlie had a grocery store with a hot dog stand in front. We still remember the delicious hot dogs with sautéed onions and the aromas of fried onions and popcorn as you approached the store. The back of the store was the family residence. Charlie's son, Jimmy, who was in his late teens had a large truck with an open back which would be filled with vegetables and fruit as he traveled the island throughout the summer selling his wares. The truck was painted in the front "Here Comes Jimmy" and in back "There Goes Jimmy". He was an excellent salesman and upon arriving in a neighborhood would give his sales pitch ending with "and strictly fresh eggs." to the housewives gathered around the truck.

Charlie Brown's

Across the street, and beyond the cement stairs (the house that belonged to the stairs burned before our time) is a private residence. In 1837, it was dismantled and moved from Cape Elizabeth by barge to its present location then rebuilt. It was the residence of the Welch family, early settlers. In our day, it was the home of one of our favorite policemen, Cy Sinnet and his wife, Hazel.

What is now the Inn on Peaks was Kenyon's garage and filling station. Before the inn was built, it had been a bakery, coffee shop, lumber store, and garage.

The shell of the Gem Theatre was still standing after a fire in 1934 destroyed the interior. The fire of 1936 completely destroyed it along with many residences and businesses on Island Avenue.

Start of the fire

The Gem fire

There was a general store at the corner of Island Avenue and Welch Street owned by Ikie and Izzy Albert. The building burned in 1936 and the Alberts relocated in town much to the islanders regret.

As we walk toward the wharf, there was a well worn path to the beach which was raked daily during the summer by volunteers. A tiny fish market was beside the path and hung out over the rocks. There were two buildings at Forest City Landing. The first was at the foot of the street and was a restaurant called "Ma Watson's". There was a lunch counter on one side and booths lined up on the other with a juke box by the door. It was a popular hangout for teenagers and our favorite. The back of the restaurant extended over the water and seemed a little shaky. The building must have been very old by then. "Ma" and her brother, Arthur, were very patient with us. If it wasn't too busy we would dance in the back, shaky floor and all, but only a few at a time.

Our waiting room, the second building, was at the end of the wharf. There was a ticket office in one corner and the main room had benches all around the room with a large pot belly stove in the center, tended dutifully by the ticket agent, Mr. McKeil or his daughter, Eleanor. It was a warm dry place to wait for the boat and the entire building was enclosed, unlike our present waiting area. Attached to this was a lunch room later used for storage and freight.

Forest City Landing

Waiting room and Ma Watson's

Reta's Uncle Sam with brother Kenneth
meeting the boat

A very large brass bell was located on the water side of the building and was rung using a hammer in foggy weather by the agent or whoever happened to be there. The boat captain would blow the whistle and steer toward the sound of the bell (no radar in those days just eyes and ears). Eunice's dad was the best in the bay. He would put his head out of the wheel house window, blow the whistle, and by the echo, knew exactly where he was. We knew we were safe when he was our captain.

Casco Bay fleet

Car Ferry Nancy Helen

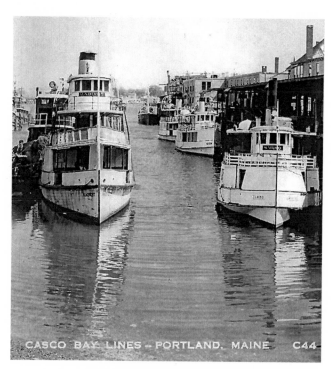

Custom House Wharf

Custom House Wharf

The car ferry slip was located between Ma Watson's and the lobster shack which is still standing. Our passenger boat fleet consisted of the Admiral, Aucocisco, Emita, Gurnet, Maquoit, Sabino and the Tourist and landed adjacent to the car ferry. The Nancy Helen was one of our car ferries. There was no car ferry service during the war.

Our memories are dim, and we just barely remember the beautiful old hotels that were located on the left side of Welch Street going towards Island Avenue. After the fires of 1934 and 1936 there were only a few small buildings. At the corner, there have been many businesses over the years, one of them an A&P grocery store. It was an ice cream shop when we were teenagers and another hangout.

The Innes House was built in 1872 on Welch Street east of Elephant Avenue now named Adams Street. A few years later it was moved down the hill then moved again 50 feet to its present location at a cost of $1 per foot. It was a summer boarding house for many years with the dining room located around the corner on Welch Street. Both now are private residences.

The American Legion building is up Welch Street beyond the Innes House. It was once a summer cottage with a large porch. The purchase by the Legion members was made possible by a donation from John Ford, the movie director and frequent summer visitor whose family had a summer cottage on the island. The post was named for two islanders, Earl Randall a World War I Marine pilot who was killed in a plane crash in 1922 and Arthur MacVane, whose submarine was lost in the Pacific during World War II. When we were young many functions were held there. Our favorite was the annual Christmas party for island children. Santa Claus was played by an islander, George Keenan, a small man, dressed as Santa, who doled out presents and candy while Irene Crandall pounded out Christmas songs on the upright piano.

Wilder Brackett lived next door to the Innes House at the corner of Island Avenue and Brackett Avenue. He had an ice pond on the southeast side of the island. In the winter the ice was cut and stored in the barn to be delivered to island homes in the summer. It was at the end of Winding Way into the woods. There is a private residence in the area now. We used to skate there after the ice was cut. It was great for skating because it was a lot larger than some of the other ponds.

Our teacher, Virginia Brackett, niece of Wilder, lived on the opposite corner with her aunt and uncle. She was everybody's favorite teacher. Looking up at the top of the hill, you can see the Brackett Homestead, built in 1820 and the second oldest house on the island. It was sawed in two and moved by oxen in 1834 from Island Avenue near the Power Company to its present location.

Archie's Café, a tavern, was on Island Avenue across from Miss Brackett's. This was a new building as the original one burned. The then owner, Gus Carlson had it rebuilt. Archie and Muriel came during the war, and it became a very popular place and a hangout for the soldiers as well as islanders. It always seemed crowded and noisy with the sound of the juke box when we walked by and intriguing but, of course, was off limits to us. Muriel was a good cook and she and Archie were well-liked. It closed shortly after the war when Archie and Muriel left the island.

Brackett's store was owned by Fred Brackett and later run by his son Dwight. It was then Howard's Market for many years and is now the Post Office. During the 30's and 40's there were seven grocery stores, two of them, seasonal. We also had two bakery trucks, milk delivery, dry cleaning service and taxi service.

The Cockeyed Gull was originally built as a garage. Reta's father told her that the building belonged to a couple who owned a house on Epp Street. Every Sunday they would dress as though going uptown or to church, but instead spent the afternoon sitting in their car inside the garage. The building was later remodeled and became the home and tearoom of Minerva Brackett (sister of Wilder Brackett). When tourists became scarce during the depression, Minnie converted it to a beauty parlor The Brackett family was very resourceful. Those of us with straight hair remember getting permanents there, sitting under the big machine which was attached to the ceiling and had long cords with curlers affixed to the ends.

Crandall's boathouse, fish market

Next was a large building, the Jensen Block, with two businesses. The first was The Carry-All-Shop owned by John Cox, his wife and sister. It was opened year-round and really did carry all. They had magazines, toys, toilet items. knickknacks, postcards, funny books, candy, school supplies, film and developing, a lending library, jewelry and silk stockings, paper dolls, etc. We children loved it.

Next door was Jensen's Grocery store, owned by Reddy and Irene Jensen. In those days, transactions were usually cash; checking accounts were uncommon and credit cards unheard of. The customers stood at the counter while the clerk walked around and selected the requested items. The clerk would list the cost and add up the total without a calculator.

The house across the street belonged to Kitty Grant, a pianist and playwright, and her brothers John and Hiram, the fiddle-player. Their house had burned in the fire of 1936 and was rebuilt. Kitty was the author of the popular play, *Rosemary of the Island*, which was presented each summer at the Brackett Memorial Church with islanders playing the roles. Kitty would advertise the upcoming event by spelling out the title with white rocks on her front lawn. A complete script has not been found since Kitty gave each performer a copy of his or her lines only.

Actress Pauline Fielding Stephens, Playwright
Kitty Grant and Hannah Payne

Our teachers, Virginia Brackett and Beatrice
Thompson with Jessie Trefethen

In our time, the post office and the doctor's office, and at times a dentist, shared the building where the launder mat is located today. Dr. Black's hospital was across the street (now apartments) and he and his wife, a registered nurse, and their staff provided medical care for a number of years. Many island children were born there, including Alice. The hospital was in operation for over twenty years and closed in the early 30's when the Blacks left the island. We were then without a doctor for many years.

During his time on the island, Dr. Black made house calls, walking before an automobile was available to him; he also traveled to the other islands, including Cliff and Jewel's by open boat. He was quoted as follows "Though I have crossed the Atlantic 14 times, I have never found a more forbidden passage as one, at times, encounters to Cliff or Jewel's Island."

The Hurdy Gurdy man with his monkey,
a frequent summer visitor

Next, on the corner of Central Avenue, was the Catholic Church rectory, now a private residence.

Across the street was Pedersen's garage owned by Reta's father, Chris, and his brother Sam. The business was started by their brother, Bill, as "Cars for Hire" and was given to Reta's dad when Bill left for college. Her father and uncle then bought the land, built the garage, expanded the business and operated Peaks Island Garage at that location for 42 years. They continued to operate the "hire" cars until the war, when gas was rationed and tires and even retreads were difficult to get. Reta remembers the fare was fifteen cents. In the summer there were four cars with the drivers working shifts from six in the morning until midnight and meeting the boats at the three boat landings, Forest City, Trefethen and Evergreen. The taxis, painted a vivid blue, met all the boats year-round, and were a welcome sight, especially on cold winter days.

Doctor's Office, Post Office and
Peaks Island Garage

Driver Ken Cameron and Peaks Island Taxis

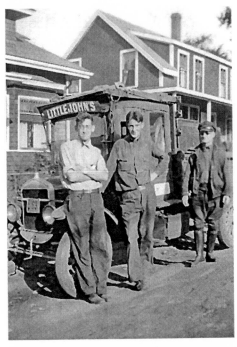

Chris, Ted Johnstone and Herman Littlejohn
(note the jodhpurs-Herman always wore them)

Jensen Block, Post Office and
Peaks Island Garage

At the garage, Chris and Sam did everything from fixing flat tires and charging batteries to replacing sparkplugs. Muffler replacement and repair were common because of the very rough, pot-holed roads. The gas pumps were on the sidewalk and Reta remembers gas at sixteen cents a gallon. The signs on each side of the large metal sliding doors were hand drawn and painted red and white as those were the Socony colors and her dad was a Socony dealer. He was also the agent for Western Union and whenever there was a telegram for an island resident or visitor who did not have a telephone, Western Union would call the garage, they in turn would drive to the residence and inform the person to contact Western Union. At that time, most summer cottages did not have telephones and there were only a few pay phones on the island. Chris received twenty-five cents per call from Western Union.

Island Avenue

Island Avenue before the fire

Winter scene before the fire

The Telephone Company was located at the corner of Island Avenue and Central Avenue. It had an old drop switchboard that had been used in the Portland office and had seven or eight positions for the operators, usually only two operators were needed at a time and only one all night operator. Some of the customers had private lines but the majority had "party" lines, some with four customers per line.

Telephone Exchange

The office was open to the public from 8 a.m. to 5 p.m., Monday through Friday, for customers to pay their bills or use the pay phone in the lobby. The pay phone was used a lot in the summer because many of the summer residents did not have telephones.

The office covered Peaks, Cushings, Little and Great Diamond and Long Islands, and the Coast Guard station at Halfway Rock. When the fire alarm sounded, there would be a flood of calls, asking where was the fire and if the operators didn't know, they would tell them whether or not the fire truck went past the office so the callers would at least know the direction of the fire truck. Also, the fire alarm signaled the general location of the fire and most of the islanders kept the coded card handy that identified the cross streets. We had volunteer firemen, just as we do now. There have been some horrendous fires on the island over the years, and the sound of the fire alarm puts us all on alert.

St. Christopher's Catholic Church, on Central Avenue, was built in 1924 on land purchased from the Littlejohn family. Before the church was built, services were held at the Greenwood Garden Dance Pavilion and later at the Gem Theatre. According to Church records, the first Mass was offered at the site of the school by a missionary priest for the local Indians. The priest, Father Sabastien Rasle, S.J. traveled with the Indians on all of their expeditions from their home in Norridgewock to Casco Bay, Saco and the Isle of Shoals.

St. Christopher's Catholic Church

Interior of St. Christopher's

Across the street from the church was the Machigonne, at one time, the summer home of Capt. John Bennett, Eunice's paternal great-grandfather. In our day, it was an apartment house. It was later torn down and replaced by St Christopher's Parish Hall. It is now a private residence.

Machigonne

Back to Island Avenue, the house across the street from the telephone company was Eunice's paternal grandfather's home. It was moved from the corner of Central Avenue to its present location and is still owned by a member of the Randall family. Next door was the only brick house on the island, at one time a doctor's office.

Island Hall was located on the site of what is now the library. It was built in 1832 and was the first permanent school building. After the school was moved to its present location, the hall was used for meetings and social gatherings of all kinds as well as the island polling place. Next door was the fire barn.

Island Hall

Fire Barn and Island Hall

Peaks Island Fire Alarm

12—Island Avenue at Brook Lane
14—Trefethen and Pleasant Avenues
15—Island and Ocean Avenues
16—Pleasant Avenue, opposite Drown's
D 115—Oaklawn
D 21—Fire Station, Island Avenue
   22—Island Avenue and Church Street
   23—Central Avenue near Oak Street
   24—Brackett Avenue and Adams Street
  25—Island Avenue and Welch Street
D 211—City Point
D 212—Knickerbocker Road
D 213—Prince Avenue and Braybrook Road
D 214—Ice House, Seashore Avenue
D 221—Tolman Heights
D 223 —Gov't. Reservation, Central Avenue
D 224—A Street opposite Pettingill's
   31—Island Avenue and Whitehead Street
   32—Seashore Avenue and Maple Street
D 311—Torrington Point
D 312—Seashore Avenue at Great Pond
D 313—Winding Way.
D 314—Spruce Avenue
D 315—Meridan and Orchard Streets
IN CASE OF FIRE TELEPHONE "707"

"Always Be Careful With Fire All Ways"

Fire box call numbers

The Avenue House was the last summer hotel in operation in our youth. Most of the clients were actors here for the season at Greenwood Garden Playhouse. Eunice worked there summers.

Avenue House

Beyond the Avenue House is the large white house on the corner of Island Avenue and Elizabeth Street that was formerly The Mansfield House, an inn, tavern, and bowling alley, built sometime after 1820, and is the third oldest house on the island. It was built by Edward Mansfield to accommodate the sailors from the sailing ships anchored nearby. In 1827 it was bought by John Sterling of House Island who changed it to a residence for his son Luther. When we were young, Harry Files and his wife, Marion, lived there and had a grocery store in the building across the street, now a private residence.

CHAPTER THREE

PEAKS ISLAND SCHOOL

THE FIRST TEACHER was Joseph Reed, the grandfather of Speaker of the House, Thomas B. Reed. Classes were held in the kitchen of the Mansfield House until the first school was built in 1832 where our library is now located. It later became Island Hall. In 1869 the current school was built. It still stands today surrounded by additions. It was built as a four room structure but only two rooms were finished. In 1914 a third room was finished and sanitary facilities were installed replacing the small brick building behind the school.

Old Peaks Island School

Our school

By the time we entered in the 1930's, there were four rooms with two grades each and a small office at the top of the stairs. Our days always started with the Pledge of Allegiance to the Flag, a patriotic song and a bible verse. In the fall, children of summer residents sometimes started school with us, then would transfer to their regular school when the summer water was turned off.

We had parties on holidays. At Christmas each room had a small tree and we made decorations. Valentine's Day was very special. Each room had a decorated box to hold our valentines; cookies and cupcakes were brought from home. Kay Doe, whose father worked for H. H. Hay, always brought their special punch for all our parties; a great favorite of ours. (Her dad was also was a photographer and took our yearly class pictures). Girls made small colorful paper May baskets to be filled with tiny candies and given as a surprise gift to our mothers or each other on the first day of May.

Our desks and seats were bolted to the floor and were adjusted as we grew. Each desk had an inkwell in the corner, filled by our janitor, Mr. Sterling . He usually carried a wrench with him in case a desk needed adjustments because of our growth. He was very kind and patient and would help us on and off with our boots in winter when we were in the early grades.

Miss Thompson, our third and fourth grade teacher, lived behind her parents' house just steps away from the school. When we did good work, we would be rewarded with a "band day". Out would come a box of bells, sticks and tambourines. We learned to play the harmonica and Kazoo while she played the piano. Her favorite poem was "If Once You Have Slept on an Island" by Rachael Field.

If once your have slept on an island
    You'll never be quite the same.
You may look as you looked the day before
    And go by the same old name.

You may bustle about in street and shop,
    You may sit at home and sew,
But you'll see blue water and wheeling gulls
    Wherever your feet may go.

You may chat with the neighbors on this and that
    And close to your fire keep,
But you'll hear ship whistle and lighthouse bell
    And tides beat through your sleep.

Oh, you won't know why and you can't say how
    Such change upon you came,
But once you have slept on an island,
    You'll never be quite the same.

On Friday afternoons the seventh grade girls went to Woolson School in Portland for sewing classes where each girl made a headband, napkins, tea towel, an apron, and a bag to put everything in. These were to be used the following year at Walker Manual Training School at our cooking classes. There we learned how to use the proper pans, measure correctly and follow recipe directions. The boys went there also to shop classes where they made cribbage boards, napkin holders and bird feeders, etc. They made lamps and learned about electricity.

Miss Brackett taught fifth and sixth grades and was also our principal. We read the "Weekly Reader", a paper written for school children, which kept us informed about current events, articles about history, geography and science.

We walked to school, went home for lunch then back again until 3:15. On school mornings breakfast was a must, usually eaten while listening to Mr. Barnard, the AAA Safety Man, on the radio. He told wonderful stories and ended the program with a safety tip.

Across the street from the school was Richardson's store, where (if we were lucky to have pennies or nickels) we could buy candy or ice cream cones. The building was originally Golden Cross Hall. Dances were held there at one time, according to Alice's father who used to chaperone the dances there.

During the war we had frequent civil defense drills. We also brought money for a savings book which when filled with stamps amounting to $18.75 was converted to a savings bond. Our school saved enough to buy an ambulance and a jeep. The soldiers brought both to the school yard and we had a ceremony. We were very proud of ourselves!

PEAKS ISLAND SCHOOL JUNE 5, 1945
PRESENTATION OF MINUTE MAN FLAG AND DEDICATION OF AMBULANCE & JEEP
PHOTO BY DOE

Award Ceremony

Mr. Reiche was the Eastern District principle and it was always a special occasion when he came to visit. He was a wonderful singer/pianist and would pound out tunes with us singing along. One of our favorites was "The Grand State of Maine."

After graduation in June, we all trooped off to Portland High School (no school buses then). Many graduates of Peaks Island Grammar School went on to be notable artists, engineers, teachers, nurses. One became an admiral and many served with distinction in the military. Joan Smith, in Ellin's class, was valedictorian of her Portland High School class. Our school always had above average students.

Reta's brother-in-law, Sonny Morrill and John Allen, Ellin's classmate. John was captured and died in a POW camp during the Korean Conflict.

BRACKETT MEMORIAL CHURCH

The Brackett Memorial Church at the top of the hill beyond the school was built in 1860-1861 and dedicated on July 25, 1861. Prior to that, services were held in the school whenever a preacher came to the island or prayer meetings were held in homes. Two prominent men, Henry Brackett and Henry Trefethen led the drive to build a church and were the first to pledge money. Others followed with money, time, labor and even loads of dirt and the beautiful white church was built on Meeting House Hill.

Brackett Memorial Church

According to Reta's Aunt Jessie Trefethen's notes on the history of the church, it had a simple white interior, the choir galley was at the entrance wall and also the organ. The pews were straight and white; each family had its own. Lighting was by kerosene lamps. A bell was installed in 1886.

In 1901, as a result of a bequest from the Henry Brackett estate, the church was remodeled and enlarged and a vestry added. It was re-dedicated as the Brackett Memorial Church in honor of the oldest name on the island. The Jones Memorial window in the church is in memory of Eliza Chamberlain who came to Peaks Island to teach in 1847. She later married William T. Jones, owner of the Union House. She taught, wrote, contributed to the intellectual growth of the island, and her daughter, Alice, who donated the window, was one of the notable teachers on the island.

Shortly after the church was built, in 1868, the members obtained land for a cemetery from Daniel Trott that became Pond Grove Cemetery at Central Avenue Extension, a very peaceful secluded spot in those days. There is also the old Brackett Cemetery at Torrington Point, the Trefethen Cemetery off Island Avenue near Oaklawn and the Olde Trott Cemetery at Upper A Street.

CHAPTER FOUR

THE WAR YEARS

THE SECOND WORLD War started in Europe in September 1939 and had been going on for over 2 years when the Japanese attacked Pearl Harbor in December of 1941. A peacetime draft had been instituted earlier in 1940, and many islanders were already serving in the military. Two shipyards were built in 1940-41 on the South Portland waterfront adjacent to Bug Light and operated around the clock. Ships were first being built for Great Britain; after war was declared both yards built Liberty ships. Throughout the war, the yards continued to launch ships at an amazing pace.

Shipyard

The war changed the island dramatically. The Government, by eminent domain, took a huge part of the island, most of the back shore and all of the houses and cottages within to establish a military base. The Army Corps of Engineers arrived in the spring of 1942 and the island started to swarm with surveyors and construction workers building the infrastructure for the army. They excavated soil for the construction sites all over the island, including Brackett Avenue, Sargent Road, the Skillings farm, where the baseball field is now, Boulder and Ledgewood Roads, and more. Some of the indentations are still there. The big pond off Seashore Avenue and Alderbrook Road was created then as well as the mounds for Battery Steel and Battery Craven; both of those areas were level before. A government wharf, barracks and associated buildings, concrete bunkers to house the big guns and a bunker (Big Daddy) for the equipment and Navy personnel to man the submarine nets in Hussey Sound were all built in record time. All of Casco Bay was ringed by submarine nets, mines and underwater detection devices. When all was in place, the soldiers arrived.

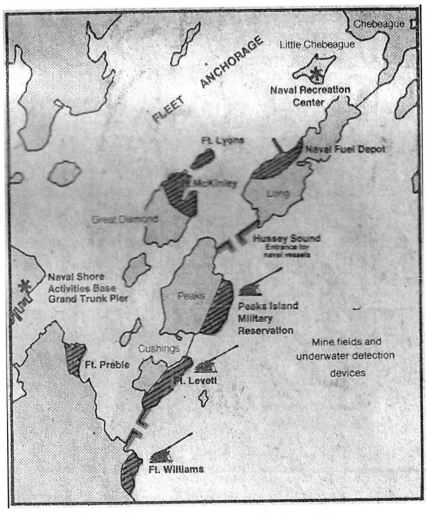

Casco Bay Military Installations, Fleet Anchorage, Mine Fields and Submarine Nets

GI's

(l) John Sims, future husband of islander, Peggy Morrill

Most of back shore was now off-limits to us. The military area was fenced and there were sentries stationed at each of the three gates. The main gate was at Brackett Avenue by the transfer station, the north gate was by Big Daddy and the south gate was by the corner of Seashore Avenue and Sandpiper Road. Blackman's farm, named Sweet Pea Farm, was one of those taken by eminent domain and was just off Seashore Avenue.

We remember a nice house with vegetable and flower gardens, high-bush blueberries, and an apple orchard in the area of Trott-Littlejohn Park that was taken over by the army, used as headquarters, and when they left all was gone. The wisteria tree which still blooms at the bottom of A Street was part of the Rand farm whose property was just inside the military line and was also taken.

Before the war, there were very few cars on the island. We walked or used Pedersen's taxi. That changed, and the traffic became busy with trucks and jeeps, especially on Brackett

Avenue since it went from the army wharf to the main gate. We got used to seeing soldiers everywhere, although not usually on our boats as they used the army boats. The *Aucocisco* was taken by the Army, painted gray (as were all of the Casco Bay Line boats) like Navy ships and renamed *Green Island* and plied between Portland, Peaks Island, Fort Preble at South Portland, Fort Levett on Cushings Island and Fort McKinley on Great Diamond along with army vessels.

The CBL *Gurnet* painted Navy Gray

Green Island and navy ships on a
cold winter day

Blackouts went into effect in the spring of 1942 when it became apparent that German submarines were using lights from the mainland to guide them in their attack on our shipping. Streetlights were covered with narrow cone beams and the tops of car headlights were painted black. Each neighborhood had an air raid warden to enforce blackout regulations. They were also trained in first aid and evacuation procedures. Their flashlights were covered with orange cellophane to dim their lights. We had dark curtains for all of the windows which had to be pulled by dusk with not a crack of light showing; otherwise the warden would be knocking at the door. Eunice's mother was the warden for her neighborhood.

Islanders had to wear identity badges to board the boats, we school children were fingerprinted and we became accustomed to the drone of the shipyards day and night.

Casco Bay became headquarters of the Navy's North Atlantic fleet and built a fuel depot on Long Island. We liked to go to the back shore in the late afternoon near the north gate at Table Rock or the rocks in front of St. Anthony By the Sea to watch the fleet come in through Hussey Sound where the Navy had submarine nets. There were ships of all sizes, from small destroyers to huge battleships. Many times the sailors would be on deck ready to go on liberty. The ships were anchored off Falmouth and the sailors going ashore were transferred to tenders for transport to the Maine State pier. When they disembarked and walked up Pearl Street, there was a sea of blue as they headed for a night on the town.

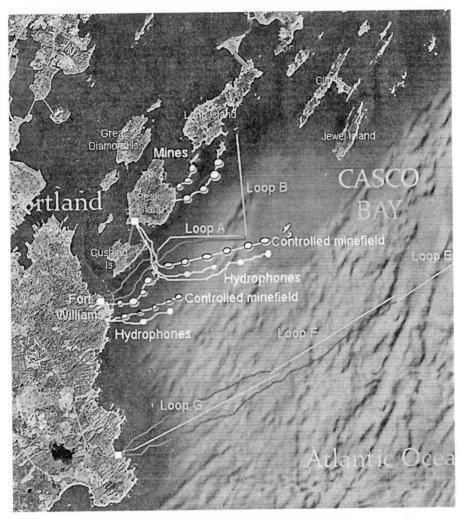

Submarine Nets and Mine Fields

Ellin remembers one night, "My mother, sister and I were walking on Pearl Street headed towards Custom House Wharf for the 5:15 boat to the island just as the sailors were headed uptown. At that time, there was a popular song titled "There're Either Too Young or Too Old" about a young woman's lament because all the young men were in the service. As we neared, one of the sailors started singing that song and it was picked up by others as we walked. Joyce and I thought it was very exciting, but our mother looked straight ahead and walked faster".

There was huge influx of workers in the Portland area and this caused a serious housing shortage. Some of the shipyard workers lived on Peaks and we had a few "Rosie the Riveters" here; recognizable by their coveralls and signature-knotted kerchiefs around the head.

Rationing began in 1942 in order to distribute scarce goods equally; in addition, price controls were established. We were issued ration books containing coupons which were dated and had to be redeemed by the effective date. There were shortages so there was no guarantee that the rationed items were available. Rationing and price controls were very complicated systems and were managed locally by War Rationing Boards. Some rationed items were fuel oil, gasoline, tires, sugar, meats, butter, oils, some cheeses, canned fruit and vegetables and their juices, dry beans, peas, lentils, processed food such as soups, baby food, baked beans and coffee. Spam was not a joke in those days; we were glad to have it as well as canned Argentine corned beef. We seldom had steak, and by the end of the war, hamburg was also scarce. Chicken, fish and eggs were not rationed nor was pasta. Rationing was probably harder on adults than children, especially meal-planning and tracking coupons.

Since butter was so scarce, oleo margarine was used instead but unlike today, margarine was white and came in a plastic see-through bag with an orange capsule. Our job, as kids, was to squeeze the capsule until it broke open then knead the whole thing until it turned yellow to resemble butter. It was better than none at all but over the years margarine has come a long way.

We witnessed the arrival of two 16-inch guns to be placed at Battery Steel. They were brought over on huge barges to the newly built government wharf then taken up Welch Street to Island Avenue to Brackett Avenue – two very difficult turns that took lots of maneuvering before they were successful. We school children were informed shortly after their installation that there would be testing on a certain day. We removed pictures and mirrors from the walls and whatever else was fragile, but all in vain. There was no test, but several months later, without any warning, they did go off. No damage was done, except a few broken windows. We, of course, were not told why they were fired, but it was rumored that there was a skirmish with German submarines.

Government Wharf

One of the two 16" guns
installed at Battery Steele

The music and movies of the era were often war-related. Jitterbugging was popular and, of course, slow dancing. Wonderful songs like "As Time Goes By", "I'll Be Seeing You", Don't Sit Under the Apple Tree". There were some wonderful movies ; who can forget *Casablanca*.

In pre-war days, women wore silk stockings made from silk imported from Asia. Of course, with world war that was unobtainable. In place, women wore hosiery made from rayon, which was saggy and ill-fitting. Any pre-war silk was saved for special occasions. Nylon was developed for parachutes and was not used for stockings until after the war.

Shoes were rationed and had to last. There were always trips to the shoe repair shop and we also had self-repair kits so we could glue the soles back on, when necessary, or pound the nails back in. Our shoes would often come unglued and the flaps would slap as we walked; that meant back to the repair kit and the glue and hope you could make it until time for the next pair of shoes. The shoes were made from synthetic leather and didn't last.

There were labor shortages everywhere. Workers left non-essential jobs for the higher-paying defense industry or other war-related work or were drafted or enlisted in the military. Wages were good, and it gave a lot of people the opportunity to recoup some of the losses of the depression.

Although the military had their own telephone system, the volume of business at the telephone office increased tremendously, as did most businesses. Several of the employees left to work in the city and two enlisted in the services, one in the army (WAACS), the other in the navy (WAVES). This created an operator shortage, especially since there was a limited work force on the island.

Mrs. Kane, the Telephone Company Agent, (Joyce and Ellin's mother) recruited homemakers who had not worked for many years, if at all. Some were reluctant, and it took a hard sell to convince them, but in the end they all enjoyed the experience. Split shifts made it convenient for them to balance home and work. There was great camaraderie among all of them.

Before the war, it was known that German Uboats were prowling the coast looking for the convoys bound for

Europe. On a late fall evening when all the summer cottages were closed up for winter, Joyce and Ellin's dad was in Johnny's, a grocery store located on the corner of Seashore and Ryefield Streets (now a private residence). A stranger entered wearing a long leather coat, spoke very little, and bought all of the bouillion cubes and candy bars. Outside the store, he turned right and continued on Seashore Avenue towards the back shore. It appeared that he arrived in a boat but we'll never know. Of course, we were convinced he was off a U-boat.

There were many spy stories, and strangers heading for the back shore were viewed suspiciously. We remember a man who used to come to the island in the winter in the pre-war days as well as the early war years. He was very conspicuous because of his large size, the full-length raccoon coat he usually wore, and the camera he carried. He would head for the back shore and we were convinced he was a German spy. We had very active imaginations fueled by the war movies we saw. We had good reason to be suspicious, because in 1944 two German spies were dropped off from a submarine at Hancock Point across Frenchman Bay from Bar Harbor. They asked for directions to town from two locals they passed, then took a taxi to the railroad station to pick up the train to New York City. They were apprehended there shortly thereafter. Earlier, in June of 1942 spies were dropped by submarine on Long Island, New York. They were also caught.

As the war winded down, civilians were allowed on the base to go to the movies, the NCO club and sometimes the Post Exchange. When the war ended, the soldiers left and for awhile there was a caretaker. Some of the barracks and other buildings were bought by islanders and moved to other locations and renovated. The remaining buildings were left to deteriorate until a fire in 1957 destroyed them. The roads were not maintained for many years, including Seashore Avenue. Despite that, we were happy to have the area open to us once again, to be free to walk everywhere and to see all of the back shore again.

The overseas edition of the Portland Press Herald.
The paper was reduced in size to 7 by 9 inches for
distribution to servicemen during the war

Barracks

Reta and friends checking out barracks
after the war

CHAPTER FIVE

NOTABLES IN OUR TIME

T HERE WERE MANY living on the island during our childhood who had an impact on our lives or became well-known. Here are a few of them.

GEORGE E STERLING

The Honorable George Sterling, Chairman of the Federal Communication Commission, FCC, was born on Peaks Island in 1894 and although the family moved to Springvale, Maine when he was 7, they returned to Peaks each year to spend the summer.

He was interested in radio at an early age and had his first wireless station at age 14, one of the first amateurs. He served in the National Guard in 1916, then as a radio operator in the Merchant Marine before serving in the infantry during World War I.

While at the front in Europe, he was commissioned as a Second Lieutenant assigned to General Pershing's headquarters in Chammount, France. He then organized a radio section for the 1ST Army Signal Corps to intercept enemy radio messages and locate their stations by direction finders. That was the beginning of a career that took him to the top of radio intelligence work.

He eventually went to work for the federal government in radio-related positions and in 1940 was appointed to head a new section of the FCC, the National Defense Operations Section (NDO). The Section was established to monitor clandestine radio operations in the United States and its possessions. The Section was later upgraded to a division becoming the Radio Intelligence Division (RID) and George became its Chief.

In 1944 George, testifying before Congress, revealed how he and his staff intercepted secret broadcasts from an illicit radio station in the German Embassy 2 days after Pearl Harbor. It caught the attention of the whole country and brought some of the details of how RID worked.

In 1948, George was nominated by President Truman and confirmed by the Senate as FCC Commissioner. He served from 1948 to 1954.

After his retirement, he and his wife spent many years at their home at Evergreen.

HERMAN LITTLEJOHN

Herman Littlejohn was born on Peaks Island in May 1914 and was a descendent of the earliest settlers of the island dating back to 1762. During his youth he was a concert violinist. At one time he accompanied crooner Rudy Vallee when his band performed at the Gem Theatre.

He served in the U. S. Navy prior to World War 2 and was assigned to the first U.S. aircraft carrier, the USS *LANGLEY*. He later joined the Federal Bureau of Investigation and retired after twenty-seven years of distinguished service. He was recruited by the General Telephone Company of Pennsylvania to create a security department and served 19 years as Security Director. Although his careers took him from Peaks, he returned often.

The Trott family of which he is a descendent owned the middle section of the island and later granted a section of land that is now Pond Grove Cemetery. Herman Avenue, Daniel Street and Ernest Street are named for family members. In later years, Herman painstakingly restored the family burial grounds, Ye Olde Trott Cemetery, on Ernest Street. The park at the foot of A Street. Trott Littlejohn Park, is named for his family.

FATHER SAMUEL DONOVAN

Father Donovan was pastor of St Christopher's Catholic Church from 1932 to 1942, much loved and respected for his many acts of kindness towards all. At that time, there was not a doctor on the island; however, Father had studied medicine on the side while studying theology so was allowed to provide medical advice to us. It was truly a godsend (especially in those pre-insurance days) and spared many of the islanders the expense of an uptown doctor. He tended to all islanders and was available whenever called upon.

Father was rarely seen without his dog, Ruggs, an Airedale or his successor Toro Taurus (who responded to Latin). Later on, Toro was succeeded by Toro Taurus Secundus.

Father was the son of Dr. Samuel Donovan, a well-known Quincy, Massachusetts, physician and his wife, Ita Welch, a noted contralto soprano. He studied in Rome then was a professor of philosophy at several colleges. He served as an Army chaplain during World War I then returned to teaching. He came to Portland and taught at Catholic Institute (the forerunner of Cheverus High School) and was appointed principle in 1921. He served in that capacity until 1932 when he was named pastor of St. Christopher's on Peaks Island. In 1942 he was transferred to St. Patricks's in Portland. He was sadly missed by the islanders.

JOHN FORD

John Ford's family had a cottage on Great Pond Road and he was a frequent visitor here. His donation enabled the American Legion members to buy and renovate a cottage on Welch Street that became Legion Hall.

John Ford was born John Feeney in Cape Elizabeth and spent his boyhood years on Munjoy Hill. He attended local schools, and while at Portland High School played football. His nickname then was "Bull Feeney". He left Portland in 1916 to join his brother, Francis Ford, in Hollywood. Francis was acting and directing in films in the fledging movie industry and became his brother's mentor in those early days.

Eventually John started directing films and became one of the most acclaimed directors in the film industry. He earned four Academy Awards for best director, a record unmatched today, and is considered by many to be Hollywood's finest. While in the U.S. Navy during World War II, he made documentaries for the Navy Department and won two more Academy Awards.

There is a statue of him at the corner of Pleasant and Danforth Streets in Portland.

THE DAVIES SISTERS

Mabel and Mary Davies were long time summer residents who were instrumental in the founding of the Trefethen-Evergreen Improvement Association in 1912. They saw a need for an island association devoted to the well-being of the island to counter the carnival atmosphere being promoted at Forest City Landing. They held the first meeting at their cottage to discuss the need of such an organization, and from that meeting the organization was created.

The Misses Davies were ardent nature lovers and transformed their back shore property into a woodland bird sanctuary. They had bought untamed Trefethen land off Seashore Avenue, built a large cottage and cleared the whole area of fallen trees and brush. They then created a forest glade with paths winding through the woods filled with wild flowers and rock formations all in their natural state. As specified in their will, their property became a bird sanctuary.

JESSIE TREFETHEN

Jessie Trefethen was a teacher, painter, author, historian and guardian of the Trefethen heritage. After her retirement from Oberlin College, where she taught art, she returned to Peaks Island to live at the Homestead, the Trefethen landmark built by her great, great grandfather. Her book *Trefethen: The Family and the Landing* tells the history of her family and the island.

CLAUDE MONTGOMERY

Claude Montgomery was an islander who became a world renowned painter; his portraits hang in galleries all over the country. He was a graduate of Peaks Island Grammar School, Portland High School, and studied at the Portland School of Fine and Applied Arts and the National Academy of Art School in New York.

In addition to portraits, he was a fine etcher as well as a watercolorist. His friends and former classmates on Peaks Island looked forward each year to his Christmas card, usually one of his seascape watercolors. His oil painting of John F. Kennedy hangs at the Harvard Club in Boston.

Claude Montgomery 1967

Christmas Card Sent to Reta's Dad

In later years, Claude and his wife, Louise (they met as children on Peaks Island) founded Friendship House in Portland, a shelter for homeless men.

CHAPTER SIX

ALICE

Alice

I WAS THE youngest of six children; one sister, the eldest and four brothers. It was a lively house with all of us, and probably noisy growing up with four brothers. Throughout the day my mother sang hymns of all kinds, and we could tell by the tone of the hymn whether she was in a happy or somber mood and so were able to determine the right time to bring up any "transgressions".

My brother Robert and I were born on Peaks Island at Dr. Black's Hospital on Island Avenue. My brother Richard was also supposed to be born there, but he arrived when the doctor was in Portland and so was born at home, delivered by my father and grandmother.

I have lived on Peaks in my family home all of my life. I have seen a lot of changes on the island in all these years, although none of them as dramatic as the changes caused by the war. The depression also had a major impact. We were too young to know what was going on, but were told that those years were very difficult for the islanders. Many of the summer visitors stopped coming here, but most of the islanders stuck it out, maybe because taxes were low in those days. My parents believed in "Yankee thrift". I remember my Dad purchased a cow, had it butchered, then rented a food locker in town where he stored it. We also had a vegetable garden and chickens.

One of my earliest recollections is when I was about 5 years old and my brother Frank called home to ask my dad to meet him at the wharf to pick up a fish Frank had caught. Dad got out his wheelbarrow, put me in it and wheeled off to the dock. When we got there, my brother loaded it onto the wheelbarrow but it was so big they had to take the sides off the wheelbarrow and I had to carry them home while dad pushed the wheelbarrow. It was too big to bring into the house, so my mother got a saw and a hatchet and cut it up in chunks. Everyone in the neighborhood had fish for dinner that day.

Reta, Eunice and Mr. Boyce

When I was little (pre-school) I loved staying home with my mother after my sister and brothers left for school. That may be why I disliked school so much. I remember in the first grade deciding to go home at recess; I would dash out the door when the bell rang and run all the way home with one of my brothers chasing after me and bringing me back. When the front door was blocked, I went out the back door. This went on for a while until the teacher finally got Richard and Robert each guarding a door to keep me in. In spite of all that, I ended up having perfect attendance all 12 years.

There was a dairy farm below us on A Street where we got our milk and vegetables. It was a beautiful spot with high bush blueberries, an apple orchard, vegetable and flower gardens. Today all that remains are beautiful wisteria vines. Blackman's farm on the back shore, called Sweet Pea Farm, was another lovely farm. It had a large apple orchard and was a great place for us kids to go in the fall to swipe apples. One time we were helping ourselves and ended up with so many apples we "borrowed" a basket to carry them home. Next day, I was returning the empty basket and got caught in the act.

There were so many natural advantages to growing up on Peaks Island. Swimming was one of my favorites. I was on the high school swimming team and wanted to enter the Peaks to Portland swim but my dad was concerned about who would row the boat that would accompany me as my brothers were all in the service. As it turned out, one of my brothers came home on leave before the race, but it was too late to enter.

Peaks to Portland Swim

Skating and sledding were also favorites. My dad kept my blades well sharpened so I was usually had one of the fastest sleds on the hill. Church Hill was our favorite, and the aim was to ride down the hill and have enough speed to make the turn down Centennial Street. I remember one ride on a toboggan and ending up in the water at the end of Centennial Street. We skated on ponds off Brackett Avenue, through the woods near what is now called the "Indian Trail". They were called Potato Pond and Carrot Pond; named before our time. The older boys determined when it was safe to skate, cleared the ponds, and watched over the younger children. We also skated on Brackett Pond and Trefethen Pond after the ice-cutting was completed. Our skating and sledding were both very much restricted once the army arrived.

Summers were spent in or on the water, rain or shine, as much as possible. I remember Eunice and I taking her Dad's punt out on the bay without his permission, rowing all over the bay, keeping out of his sight. He finally realized what we were doing so he then painted the punt a bright blue, and with his sharp eyes he was able to spot it anywhere.

Tolman Heights was one of our special places with its windmill and Whitney's tower. The two Tolman sisters were island favorites. I never had the pleasure of having May as a teacher, but I know all of her high school students loved her. She greeted them each day saying "Good morning my little folksies". Their father, a judge in Westbrook, had bought the land years before.

It seemed as though the island changed overnight when hordes of men (surveyors, construction workers, etc.) arrived one day, streamed off the boat and headed up Brackett Avenue. We heard that the Army was going to build something on the "reservation", a small bit of Army land off Central Avenue extension with a World War 1 searchlight on it. Before long, a large part of the island was fenced in and off limits to us.

We watched the sixteen inch guns being brought here via barge to the new Army wharf and held our breath as we watched them trying to make the turns onto Island Avenue and then the even more difficult turn onto Brackett Avenue. We soon got used to seeing soldiers everywhere. My four brothers were all in the service during the war; Frederick, the oldest, was in the Army, Frank was in the Navy, Richard was in the Air Force, and Bob was in the Navy. Frank was stationed on a destroyer that came into Casco Bay for refueling (at the Navy fuel depot on Long Island). He called home, but was unable to tell them just how close he was to them. Later on, both his ship and Bob's were in port in the South Pacific and they were able to meet.

One Sunday afternoon Richard called home just before he was due to be shipped out. My Dad answered and told him to call back later as Mom was at church but he was unable to call again. The island operator on duty recognized the voice of her favorite paper boy, came in on the line and told him to wait as she had just seen Mom heading towards Cox's Carry-All Shop. She called John Cox and told him to bring Mom into the shop to pick up the call on the pay telephone there. Thanks to the operator Richard, Mom and Dad had their conversation.

On Saturday mornings the soldiers had maneuvers at the water tower at the top of Brackett Avenue: one army defending it, the other trying to capture it. Mother had a huge coffee pot, always filled, on the old Queen Atlantic coal stove and homemade donuts. She and Dad would invite the soldiers in when they finished to get warm and have some coffee and donuts. Since all four of the Boyce boys were away from home in the military, Dad and Mom hoped people would be kind to them.

Many of the island men and boys served in the military during the war. Several of the boys left high school to sign up and because they were under-age, needed parental consent. After the war, they went back to school to get their diplomas and several of them took advantage of the GI Bill to get a college education. After the war it was not unusual to see 20 and 21 year olds walking the halls of Portland High School. Several pretty English war brides arrived here after the war ended. There was also a vivacious Russian bride, who had served in the Russian Army and, according to her husband, could field strip a gun faster than he could.

Auxiliary President Ethel MacVane and Commander Cyril Hill in front of the monument honoring Islanders who served in the military in WWII.

The Emita, our school boat

Alice and Eunice meeting the boat

Picture-taking was forbidden in certain areas. A friend of ours who grew up on Peaks came to visit his parents, our next door neighbors. He brought with him a camera and went to the back shore to take some pictures. He hadn't gotten very far when he was apprehended by the MP's who confiscated his camera and took him to the police at the fire barn to await transfer to Portland. The police there were able to identify him as the son of the then Fire Chief on Peaks. After he was identified, he was released. He did get his camera back, but not his film.

When the war was in its final stages, we were allowed onto the military reservation to go to the movies. There were two shows a night and we kids went to the early show. Harold Clark, who had a big delivery van, would pick us up Down Front and take us to and from the movie. It was a real treat to see a movie on the island instead of having to go uptown. Also, the movies were first-run and would not be shown in Portland for months.

For a short time after the war, we had bus service on the island. One night, on the way to the movies, the bus hit a soft shoulder on Brackett Avenue and one of the passengers, Eleanor McKeil, our Casco Bay Lines ticket agent, was killed. Shortly after that the bus service ended.

During the 30's and 40's the island had a very successful baseball team. Before the war, the ballpark was near Brackett Avenue and A Streets. Playing was suspended for the duration of the war and then resumed for a few years in the late 40's.

We saw a lot of people come and a lot of people go. One of these was a fugitive from justice who was on the ten most wanted list. His name was O'Dell (dubbed Digger O'Dell by the locals). He lived near Casco Bay Power Company. He had a job in town and for whatever reason (to be inconspicuous?) walked back and forth from the boat by way of the beach. Since newcomers were more of a rarity then, he was already being noticed and avoiding Island Avenue only made people more suspicious of him. Finally the long arm of the law caught up with him after an islander saw his picture in a detective magazine and notified the authorities.

Few people owned automobiles in the 30's and 40's. This was not only true on the island but also in Portland. Most of the residents relied on public transportation. I remember as a child riding on the electric trolley cars, later replaced by buses.

The railroad was the prime means of travel when going outside of Portland. Reta remembers taking the train to Old Orchard Beach each summer with her parents. Union Station on St. John's Street was one of the most beautiful buildings in the state and also one of the busiest, especially during the war. It was filled with servicemen and women and their loved ones either seeing them off or welcoming them home.

Grand Trunk Station with service between Portland and Canada was located on the corner of Commercial and India Streets with the track running the length of Commercial Street. Today we see lots of traffic along the waterfront but it is nothing compared to coming down Pearl Street (the boats left from Custom House Wharf then) only to see box cars at a dead stop and lined up with seemingly no beginning and no end and not much time to catch the boat. This happened to me occasionally. I remember walking a half mile or so out of my way, then running like mad to the wharf. I was lucky, I only missed the boat once. Some of the more adventurous of us would jump over the couplings which was very dangerous.

Island living isn't for everyone but it sure suits me. Someone asked me recently if I have lived here all of my life. "No" I answered, "Just up until now".

CHAPTER SEVEN

EUNICE

Eunice

I WAS THE second of three daughters, Marilyn Frances was the eldest and Annie was the youngest. I am a direct descendant of George Cleeves and Michael Mitton, founders of Portland, through both the Haggett and Bracket lineages. My appearance on this island was in the fall of 1930 on Luther Street in the home of my parents, George Clifford and Frances Haggett Randall. In those early morning hours, my mom's doctor failed to show up, so I was delivered by my grandmother, Annie Bennett Randall and Mae Copeland, a nurse who at that time lived in the house I've owned and lived in for over fifty years.

My father was born on Peaks Island and spent his youth on the waters of Casco Bay. He married Frances Haggett of South Portland, a reporter for the *Portland Press Herald* for eighteen years. In later years, she became blind from diabetes. Dad was a Stationary Engineer at the Immigration Hospital, now a pile of rubble behind the shore dinner cookhouse, on House Island. He was then Captain on the Steam Vessel *Sabino* for more than 30 years on the late run out of Casco Bay Lines. He routinely ran between Peaks Island and Portland.

Capt. Cliff Randall

Dad was one of a kind. Before returning to Casco Bay Lines after midnight, he would tie SV *Sabino* up in the lee of Diamond Island at the old Navy Fuel Depot. He would row over to Peaks to make sure we were warm and dry. He would then row back and take the *Sabino* to the city. He would come home in the morning and bake muffins, cook oatmeal or bacon and eggs for us before we went to school.

Dad was one of the first skippers in the bay to have female deck hands. For several summers, 3 sisters, Ellen, Joan and Marie Zukunft, worked summers on the *Sabino*. It would be many more years before there was another female crew.

Capt. Cliff and Joan Zukunft

My sisters and I had pet ducks, Skippy and Spooky. They were scheduled to appear on the menu at the Randall home once they achieved the proper weight. Once we realized their fate and Skippy was prepared to adorn our dinner table, we three girls set up a howl that could be heard in Canada. Our dad quickly removed our pet to our grandparents house.

One of my earliest memories was on a June day in 1936 when I was five years old. My mother had taken my sisters and me to visit dad's cousin, Ben Randall and his wife, Edith and their two daughters, Flora and Roberta (the author of *Experiences of My Early Life On House Island In Casco Bay*). They lived just up the street from us. We were going home when we smelled an acrid odor and smoke drifted over the island. There was a bucket-brigade at almost every house. The flames hop-scotched over the houses, taking one and leaving the one next door. My sisters and I watched the houses across the street burn next to the Telephone Company office. My Aunt Esther gave me a teddy bear to hold to shut me up. Many houses and businesses were burned to the ground that day. Many empty lots and gaping holes remained for years. The smoke hung over the island for days! The fire was caused by someone burning leaves on Torrington Point and the wind came up. There's a lesson here.

We children didn't have TV sets or any of the modern amusements they have today. We played kick the can, hopscotch and hide and seek. We swam in the summer and rowed. We skated in the winter.

Then the war came. We watched the Corps of Engineers build the Army Wharf, Battery Steel and Battery Craven. The gravel pit which adjoins my land on Ledgewood Road was excavated by the Corps and gave us many hours of watching as our neighbor, friend and babysitter, Bernadette, sat on a huge earthmover and did her version of "Rosie the Riveter". I was convinced that I wanted to be a driver like her when I grew up!

We were prevented from going on the military reservation for most of the war for security reasons, eventually however, we were allowed and every Friday night we (kids and adults) would gather to hop aboard a vehicle that was going to the movies on the base. We were allowed to go to the early show. We saw feature films before the rest of the nation saw them. Eventually we were allowed to take our bicycles on the reservation. There were neat streets and barracks and the military had quite a complex on the back shore. There were several gates guarded by Army personnel.

Then there were my babysitting experiences, mostly for Bernie and many of the military families. Bernie lived across the street. We loved her and her kids. Bernie babysat my sisters and me when we were small. There were many babysitting opportunities with all the young military families assigned to the batteries.

I remember the time Annie and her friend, Sissie who lived next door, were babysitting one afternoon. They cooked fudge and pudding using rationed sugar, which was precious and obtained only with the ration coupons at the time, as were butter, shortening to name a few. Bernie came home and discovered what they were doing and chased them out of the house, yelling at them. I later heard her tell my mother, "They didn't just use my sugar. They grabbed the fudge pan and took it home with them."

On snowy winter days when we couldn't go outdoors, my Mother would make taffy for us to pull, then she would cut it into pieces to harden so we could eat it. We had a good-sized ice-cream maker and we would go and gather icicles and make our own ice-cream. My favorite and also Annie's was pineapple sherbet. We searched all our adult life for the sherbet that equaled Mom's but found only one place that came anywhere near it. The Brighton Avenue Pharmacy (now closed).

Mama played the piano (also the violin and other instruments) and Dad played the mandolin. We would all sing my Mother's favorite hymns and my Dads favorite Irish songs. Later in life, the Catholic Priest and some of the Sisters from the convent would gather at our house for what they called their "jam session". It sure was ecumenical.

My Dad would bring home whole fish from the draggers docked alongside the Casco Bay Lines pier, such as haddock, cod, etc. One time he was given a huge lobster caught in their net. He brought it home and put it down on the kitchen floor where it proceeded to crawl across the floor. In order to cook it he had to use a canning kettle and cook the claw end first then the tail end. Needless to say it was tougher than tripe. Dad ground up the meat and froze it and tried all winter to get us to eat it in sandwiches.

Dad and His Lobster

Outside of his regular job as skipper on the *Sabino* he put out a number of lobster traps. We always had lobster and crabs aplenty. Marilyn and Annie were most appreciative but, I never developed a liking for seafood. My Grandfather, George W. Randall, had a large wharf where we all went swimming. Their house, where my Dad and his siblings were all born, is the white house across from the northwest corner of Island and Central Avenues. The house was bought from the Littlejohns and moved from the southwest corner of Island and Central Avenues.

My grandfather took fishing parties deep sea fishing in his sloop, *The Breeze*. Many prominent people, including judges and senators, went year after year. The wharf was washed out in the hurricane of 1947. My paternal great-grandfather, Capt. John Bennett was a master mariner who skippered steamships to and from New York City.

Capt. George Randall

The Breeze

Grandfather's wharf

Capt. and Mrs. Bennett

Capt. Bennett's ship, *Cottage City*

Another fond memory is when Carmie, myself, a couple of Nutters and Skippy Richards would buy a pound of butter and sit on the stairs across from the Peaks Island House Restaurant and wait for the fresh bread to come out of the oven at Don's Bakery. Don and Kitty Bartlett ran the bakery across from the stairs which are all that was left of a house after the big fire. Then we'd go into Greenwood Gardens and sit in the gazebo singing and being teenagers. Officer Leo Sinnet would saunter by and say, "That's enough for tonight."

Then at sixteen, I got a summer job at the Avenue House as a desk clerk. My job was composing menus, answering the phone and greeting check-ins. It was most interesting since the clientele was mostly actors from the summer stock theatre appearing at Greenwood Garden Playhouse, now known as the Lion's Club. Among the actors and actresses were Rod Stieger, Diana Barrymore, Efram Zimberlist Jr., Miriam Hopkins and many more who went on to fame and fortune. Rod Stieger was in "The Hasty Heart". Down in the Valley", and "Hay Fever". I have playbills for these shows. Rod Stieger would rehearse in the lobby by getting on his knees and singing to me. He had a voice which alone could have brought him fame. He only sang in one movie, "Oklahoma". Of course, he was only twenty-four years old at the time and hadn't yet achieved his fame!

Diana Barrymore, on her arrival, allowed me to carry a suitcase to her room on the second floor. She kept turning around and telling me to be careful with her "records". When we reached her room, she threw the case on the bed to examine the contents. It contained bourbon! The next morning she appeared at my desk with an armful of clothing which she shoved at me, saying "Iron these". I shoved them right back and told her to iron them herself, I wasn't hired to iron her clothes. She reported me to Henry Hoar, the owner of the Avenue House. Henry told her I was right, he didn't hire me to iron anyone's clothes! She left shortly after for accommodations on Brackett Avenue.

Miriam Hopkins appeared in the dining room in a bikini bathing suit. Mr. Hoar told her that wasn't appropriate attire for the dining room. Ethel MacVane was passing by with a tray of lobster dinners. Hopkins was so angry she tipped the tray up and dumped all the dinners on the floor. She too headed for Brackett Avenue!

My fondest memory is of the day in June 1945 when I graduated from Peaks Island Grammar School. Yes, I know the initials spell PIGS. It was a beautiful day with fluffy clouds and the water was warm enough to go swimming. Although I was happy to be out of school, I was apprehensive about going to the mainland to the big school, Portland High! Many of the city kids came to the island summers and knew we were islanders. We were asked, "Did you haul your traps this morning?" "Did you get seasick coming over?" and other taunts. It was all good natured and we soon got used to it!

We had lots of fun growing up on the island, with many of our experiences very different from our mainland contemporaries. I have lived on Peaks all of my life and cannot imagine living anywhere else.

CHAPTER EIGHT

ELLIN

Ellin

OUR GRANDPARENTS, MARY and Timothy Kane, started spending summers on Winding Way in the early 1900's. When they first started coming to the island, they stayed in a tent as did many of their neighbors. As shown in early pictures, the tent was large and rested on a platform and appeared to be sturdy. They spent several summers there before building a cottage and buying the one next to it.

Our grandmother and uncle

Our pre-school days were spent on that side of the island in a house across the street from our grandparents. In the summer it was a bustling neighborhood with lots of summer people back to their cottages; many of the same families are still returning each summer. In those days, most cottages had a front porch and there was a lot of visiting back and forth, sitting and rocking on each other's porches. There was no television, Boston Red Sox and Boston Braves games were played in the afternoons and were broadcast on the radio, and air-conditioning was unheard of.

We were the youngest children in the neighborhood, and got a lot of attention. Joyce and I were probably little pests, but we were always welcomed as we made our round of visits. Mrs. Cotton had a bakery at the top of Winding Way and was renowned for her wonderful baked goods. She was somewhat sharp-tongued, so we were a bit wary of her.

The Feeney's, John Ford's father, sister, and granddaughter lived below and around the corner from us. My grandmother and Mr. Feeney came from the same town in Ireland and Nana was friends with him and his daughters. Their house was high on our list of stops. I remember family members coming and going all during the summer, and a fun place to visit. John Ford and his brother, Frank, were there often. Frank was usually in John's movies playing a loveable old man; although, according to our mother, he was a leading man playing romantic roles in earlier movies.

Our neighbor, John Feeney, Joyce and
Ellin's parents

We spent most of our time with our neighbors across the street, the Ballard girls, Betty, Margie, and Mary. We followed them everywhere. Their mother, Fanny took us to the beach, taught us how to swim, took us on nature walks through the woods, pointing out the various wildflowers etc. She loved the island and made us aware of the natural beauty surrounding us. The family had two houses on their property; the one closest to the street was an old cottage, always called "The Camp". It was typical of many cottages on the island built in the 1890's-1900's'ie; built like a railroad car. The front room had an organ which Betty played, usually on rainy days. My favorite song was "When the Deep Purple Falls". In later life, Betty became an accomplished artist and displayed her talent early when she would sketch and paint paper dolls for us.

On sunny days we were usually at what we called Rocky Beach (its real name is Woodlanding Cove, no one ever called it that) at the end of Great Pond Road. The rocks on either side of the cove are wonderful for climbing, make great picnic tables and, of course, sunning. I've never liked sandy beaches, going for a swim and drying off on a rock is so much nicer than getting wet sand everywhere. Around the corner from the beach at low tide there is a large tidal pool with a beautiful pink floor. We called it our swimming pool and reached it by climbing gingerly over wet seaweed and barnacle-covered rocks but it was worth it.

The Ballard girls uncle had a sail boat and occasionally he and our uncles used to go dulsing. Dulse is an edible seaweed (algae) found in the North Atlantic on both coasts on rocks at low tide, it is then sun-dried and may be stored. It is very nutritious and can be found at some fish markets and health food stores; it is still harvested in Nova Scotia and can be ordered on-line. We buy it in St John's, NB, whenever we go that way. When we were children, we always knew when Nana had fresh dulse because we would recognize the pleasant smell of salt and ocean in the cottage. Sometimes at very low tide, we would find beds of it growing on the rocks farther out. Big crabs used to be closer to the shore and we had to watch out for them. A toe might be a tempting target

Our mother used to take us Down Front to Cox's Carry-All Shop to check out their lending library and to buy paper dolls, our favorites. We spent hours playing with them and I still nostalgically remember some of them. The store had something for everyone and was aptly named. When I was 6 or 7, I remember seeing a comb and case set in my favorite color of purple for 19 cents. My uncle was spending a week at the family cottage so I offered to be his "housekeeper" for the week. At the end of the week when he asked how much he owed me, I promptly replied 19 cents and so got my purple comb set.

During the winter months we were the only children in the neighborhood, so when we moved to Central Avenue it opened up a new world for us. By then we were going to grammar school. It was a four room schoolhouse with two grades (grades one through eight) to a room; Joyce and I are a year apart so every other year we were in the same classroom. We graduated with most of the children we started with in the first grade. It was quite a transition going to high school in the city after our somewhat sheltered grammar school days.

A walk in the woods to Brackett pond
and ice house.

Most of our homes were heated with coal and in the fall the coal trucks came to the island to make their deliveries. They filled our coal bins with enough coal to last until spring. My mother tended the furnace while my father was in the service. I remember watching her shoveling coal, stoking it, empting the ashes, etc. She did a good job and kept us warm and comfortable. The old slogan or lines from a song "keep the home fires burning" comes to mind. Our kitchen had a black oil burner that kept the kitchen warm and toasty. After the war, most furnaces were converted to oil.

The first family car I remember was a coupe with a rumble seat. For those who are unfamiliar with rumble seats, it was an enclosed two-seater in front with two seats where the trunk usually is and only accessible outside the car. Sort of like a back seat convertible. Joyce and I loved riding in the rumble, but obviously it was impractical and was replaced with a sedate sedan.

Saturdays our mother would take us to Portland "uptown". We would usually walk to Congress Street, then the shopping center of town, and shop a bit, lunch, then go to the movies. In those days the show consisted of a feature film, a "B" film, cartoons, previews, and a news' film. The timing of the show didn't matter to our mother, so we usually went in the middle of the feature movie then saw all of the others and the first part of the feature. If we were lucky, we wouldn't have to leave for the 5:15 boat until it had reached the point where we had come in. I was well in my teens before I saw a feature film from start to finish.

Joyce and I stopped in the telephone office on our way home each school day and when we were younger stayed there until our mother finished work. The office had a small lounge where we would wait, spending the time looking at the latest magazines. After the office was closed to customers, we would sit at the closed positions at the switchboard and play "operator". We were fully trained by the time we were old enough for summer jobs.

I worked as an operator for 2 summers, 1946 and 1947, while I was in high school. After years of playing at it, I enjoyed actually saying "Number Please" to a real person. I still remember the first fire alarm, and the feeling of helplessness I felt when it appeared every subscriber was calling in at the same time. Most of the callers were asking us if we knew where the fire was located.

I liked to take the calls from the Coast Guard station at Half Way Rock. The sailors there were always seemed cheerful in spite of being stationed on that barren rock. The lighthouse is on a windswept ledge over 10 miles from Portland. It was built in the 1870's and, until the 1970 when it was automated, was manned by 2 or 3 men. The lighthouse is 1 of 4 that can be seen from the back shore. The others are Ram Island Light, Portland Head Light, and Two Lights.

Half Way Rock

I lived "away" for many years but my heart was always on Peaks Island. I consider myself very fortunate to be home again.

CHAPTER NINE

RETA

Reta

I AM A fifth generation islander; my paternal Trefethen ancestors came from Kittery to Monhegan Island to House Island and then to Peaks Island. I was born at home on Peaks Island in the Trefethen/Walker house on the corner of Island Avenue. My Aunt Cal, a nurse, and Dr. Black (our island doctor) attended. It was the night of the first American Legion Women's Auxiliary Installation, a much anticipated social event.

In the summer, I am often asked many questions such as, "How long have you lived here?". Immediately the answer is "I was born here just over the street". "Oh! Then did you go to Peaks Island School?" "Yes, all eight grades". "What did you do for entertainment and how about emergencies"? Every so often someone will say that their grandparents or other relatives lived here and did I know them. Or someone lived here many years ago and they have come back to see how it has changed.

Mom and Dad married in 1930. By then, in addition to his taxi business, Dad and his brother, Sam had started a business together, Peaks Island Garage. They served the islanders at that location for forty-three years. I spent a lot of time at the garage as I was growing up. I remember entering the garage by the big door and looking up to see the "Old Town" canoe resting upside down on the beams, the outside painted green with shiny varnished seats, paddles tucked in. The smell of kerosene permeated everything. During the war gas was rationed and government-issued stamps were needed to buy gas. One of my jobs was to paste the stamps on large sheets so that Dad could redeem them.

Dad

After the taxis were no longer useable for passenger service, Dad would remove the back seat, cut open the back, put in a wooden platform and use the cars as trucks: Yankee frugality and ingenuity! He did all of his own bookkeeping at home. Sales were all cash and carry. I remember his money bag, made by my mother out of muslin with a drawstring. There was no cash register or cash box, no such thing as a credit card. In those days, he didn't have a checking account so paid his bills by money order or cash.

We moved to Epp Street when I was about a year and a half. One morning my mother checked on me and saw that I was sleeping soundly so she decided to run a quick errand to Brackett's store across the street. Somehow I got out of bed and went looking for her. I wandered down the street and Reddy Jensen came out of his store and spotted me. I guess I was crying and he took me to my dad at the garage. Dad took me home and mum was already there by then. I don't know what took place, but I can imagine. But I believe it was many years before my mother ever left the house without me.

In the winter, my mother would wrap me all up and put me on a sled. Dad had made sides and a back for it and off we would go, maybe to my Grammy's or one of my aunts or the sewing circle at the other end of the island. The ladies got together at Wilma Sterling's or Gladys Sterling's or Helen Knight's or Mrs. Weaver's. At one of the houses, there was a little rocking chair and my mother gave me a piece of cloth and needle and thread. I did basting and learned to sew a button on the cloth. Later I did a dish towel and gave it to Grammy. Years later she gave it back to me.

At Grammy's house there was always molasses or oatmeal cookies in a large crock in the big cupboard in the kitchen and usually a pie, usually a blackberry or blueberry in season. There was a garden that produced well so there was canning done in late summer. There were lots of shelves in the cellar to hold the canned produce; lots of pickles, a crock with sand held carrots, potatoes and maybe turnips.

Webber's store was on the corner and an apple orchard was across the street. Grammy would gather apples in her apron for pies, turnovers, cobbler, or applesauce. Grammy told me that at one time there were many fruit orchards, vegetable gardens, and strawberry and raspberry patches in the neighborhood. According to Aunt Jessie, there were crabapple trees along the street with picnic tables beneath.

Grandma Pedersen's house

In 1936 we moved to Central Avenue to the house where I now live. Only one bedroom was finished off, so Dad finished another for me, put up wallboard, laid a floor, and after all the work was done bought me a three piece bedroom set including a vanity bench. I felt like a princess. I still have the set.

In March 1937, Aunt Cal, my father's sister, came to take care of me. Mom was in town with a friend. We went to see her and the next day Aunt Cal told me I had a baby brother. I was excited, then wanted to tell my next door neighbor whose name was Mrs. Millard. I ran through the house, out the back door to her back door. "Mrs. Lard, Mrs. Lard, I have a brand new baby brother and nobody has ever had him before." She never forgot it and told me about many times.

Kenneth and Reta

May 4, 1937

Reta, her parents and brother.

That fall I started school. Joyce was in my class along with one other girl and four boys. We walked to and from school, went home to lunch then back to school until 3:15.

We had "good clothes" and "play clothes" (usually last year's "good") and changed clothes coming home from school before going out to play. Our mothers' washed, starched, and ironed our dresses and blouses and often times knitted our sweaters. We were careful with our shoes, especially during the war when they were rationed. Doing the laundry was a tedious process and involved wheeling the washing machine (a big green "Easy) to the laundry sink and hooking it up to the faucets. After washing and rinsing, everything was hand-fed through the wringer. Hopefully it was a sunny day the wash could then be hung out on the line to dry. After that came the ironing!

Before we got refrigerators (which were unobtainable during the war) we had ice boxes. Ice was not delivered in the cold months, so perishables were kept in the cold room. In the winter, my mother used to set a bowl of jello in the snow to jell. It was a familiar sight to come home from school and see the jello by the porch.

I remember watching ice-cutting on Brackett and Trefethen Ponds during the winter. It was a major undertaking and required just about every man and boy on the island to get the job done.

The ice-house had three levels. When the ice was thick enough for cutting, it was scored across the pond, then cut into large pieces. The timing was critical so that the ice was the right thickness and thoroughly frozen.

The men had long poles with hooks to guide the cakes. Arthur Ross (Rossie, our garbage-man) worked the controls to the lift. The cakes were then hoisted up to the "house". Hay was put on top of the cakes to keep them frozen. Many cakes were missed and ended up in a pile at the end of the ramp. I remember getting ice to put in our hand-cranked ice-cream maker. When warm weather returned, the ice man delivered door to door leaving the size requested as shown on the "Ice Card" placed in the customer's window.

Trefethen Pond

Cutting the ice

Shoveling crew

Our trips off the island were rare. Dad worked seven days a week and took only 1 week a year for deer hunting. Also, I got car sick. It required days of planning to visit my Grandfather Hills (my mother's father) at his farm in West Buxton. He was born in the house and passed away there the day before his 97th birthday, Christmas Day. His first wife, my mother's mother, died when she was seven years old. He remarried many years later to a schoolteacher. He never drove a car, but she did drive and they went to Farmers' market in Portland every week in season to sell their produce. I remember a large kitchen with a big black stove and a slate sink with a hand pump to pump the water from the well. The dining room had a pot belly stove. Grampa was usually there sitting in his rocker when we visited. The Farmer's Almanac hung on the wall and there were always many magazines around. There was a formal living room and another room off the dining room that was later made into a bathroom. I do remember going out through a shed toward the barn to the "two-holer."

My Grandfather 's house in Buxton

They had chickens, cows, horses, pigs and made their own butter. They also had a large garden and grew lots of flowers. They were very self-sufficient. After my grandfather's death, the farm was sold.

My father's mother, Grace and her sister, Jessie were both born in the Trefethen homestead and Jessie lived there after her retirement. She was the family historian and custodian of the Trefethen heirlooms.

Painting of Trefethen Landing that hung
at the Homestead

Reta's Aunt and Grandmother
at Trefethen Beach

My grandmother and Aunt Jessie often told me stories about the family and growing up on the island. One of the stories was about Thomas Brackett Reed. His grandmother Trefethen used to rock him in her old yellow rocker (made by Aunt Jessie's great grandfather for his house on House Island) in the study of the Trefethen homestead, and tell him that one day he would be President of the United States. It almost came to pass. The rocking chair now sits in the Peaks Island Room at the Fifth Maine Community Building.

At one time Trefethen Landing was the longest wharf on the Maine coast extending well out into the channel because the bay is very shallow on our side of Diamond Passage. Sections of the wharf had been swept away by winter storms, but were always rebuilt until the blizzard of 1959 when most of the pilings were destroyed.

The following article is taken from an old undated newspaper clipping from my mother's archives.

"A compromise has been effected in the matter of the waiting room at Trefethen Landing, Peaks Island. The Casco Bay Company has erected the building but has cut off the corner so that the view of Captain Trefethen is unobstructed."

Waiting room, Trefethen Landing,
note notch in roof

This "trip down memory lane" would not have been possible without all of the Peaks Island memorabilia collected by my parents and the wonderful stories handed down to me.

CHAPTER TEN

JOYCE

Joyce

THE CAREFREE DAYS spent at Rocky Beach are among my earliest memories. We went there every day, weather permitting. Our neighborhood had many summer residents, old and young, and many of them would show up to spend the day at the cove. Often we would have what is now called a cookout.

Someone would build a bonfire (permitted then) and out would come all sorts of food from picnic baskets. I remember helping my grandmother while she cooked one of her specialties in her large old black frying pan. She was a wonderful cook and taught my mother, her daughter-in-law, how to cook. She had a large vegetable garden; her dinner table was always covered with steaming fresh vegetables. Nana also had a hen house with chickens at the end of her garden.

One day our Dad brought home the sweetest little puppy, a wire-haired fox terrier. He was named "Deacon" by his previous owners because he was the quietest and most timid of the litter. He was an angel with us, but outside he was a street devil, so we kept him close to home. He loved to chase cars. There was not much traffic in those days but when he heard a car approaching, off he went so it was not long before a car hit him and broke his leg. We were heartbroken. There was not a veterinarian on the island, so Mother called Father Donovan. He came to the house with his little black bag and made a splint out of some pieces of wood and bandaged it. Deacon soon recovered.

Deacon

I vaguely remember the fire of 1936. My sister and I were with our grandfather as both our parents were at the telephone office. Our mother gave instructions to row us over to Cushings Island if the fire came our way. Many people in Portland watched it from the Eastern Promenade – among them my mother's manager. It looked to those watching like an inferno, as if the whole island was on fire.

All the telephone operators were on duty as the flames swept over the front of the island. Our father was on the roof with water buckets keeping it wet. The employees later received the Telephone Company's Vail Medal of Honor Award for bravery. A company banquet was also held in their honor.

The following is quoted from Telephone Topics of July 1936 newsletter.

"The Agent, five operators and the husband of the Agent at Peaks Island, Maine, fulfilled their duties in a manner that won the acclaim of a large part of New England on June 3 when a general conflagration among the wooden summer homes on the island destroyed 25 buildings and threatened to wipe out the exchange office where they were at work. Although the intense heat of the burning buildings scorched the sides of the exchange, and although the roof was showered with sparks and embers, Mrs. Margaret Joyce Kane, the Agent, and her operators valiantly remained at their switchboard calling for help and the emergency calls to Portland and to other points to the island.

William F. Kane, Mrs. Kane's husband, remained on the roof, extinguishing the blazes started by sparks and falling embers. He is a former Plant employee."

Joyce and Ellin's father, insert, and mother, standing at right
Operators (l to r) Althea Staples, Ruth Brackett, Ruth Smith, Doris O'Hara

Because of the depression most people were very thrifty in those days. Many of my clothes were hand-me-downs from Ellin, a year older than I. One fall day my mother brought home from town the prettiest snow suit I had ever seen. As I was admiring it, Mum said she was glad I liked it because it would be mine next year. Our elderly neighbor, Mr. York, a very practical man, had built his house using old trolley car parts. All of the windows on his sun porch were trolley car windows.

A plentiful source of firewood or even building material could be found at the shore. It was an island custom to place a rock on top of driftwood to indicate that it was spoken for. One day my uncle was walking along the shore the day after a hurricane. The sea was turbulent and filled with debris. He saw a swimmer in the water pushing a huge log to shore and commented to his friend how could anyone be so brave to be out there when he recognized our grandmother. I'm sure she placed a rock on the log once she got it ashore.

There is a stonewall on Seashore Avenue just as it turns by the Eighth Maine building. It has been repaired in places over the years but part of it remains as it was when we were kids when the man who lived across the street cemented pointed rocks on top of it to keep lovers from sitting on it. Our favorite stonewall is further along on Seashore Avenue.

Joyce and Ellin

We had several grocery stores all over the island. There were bakeries also. The very best was Andy Englund's Bakery, a tiny building at the corner of Whitehead Street and Seashore Avenue. All he baked was doughnuts and they were wonderful. He lived across the street in Summer Retreat with his wife, a niece of Sadie Torrington. He loved making doughnuts and they were so popular he usually sold out quickly; sometimes still warm from the oven.

During the war there were often many ships anchored in the harbor, some of them very close to Peaks. One day when Eunice and I were about twelve years old, we stopped in front of Jones Landing to watch one ship float very close to the wharf. There were two sailors at the stern and we suddenly realized they were trying to get our attention. They disappeared for a short time, then came back and threw something overboard.

By this time the ship was beginning to drift away with the tide and as we scrambled down to the beach we saw a bottle coming to shore. To our amazement, we found a note inside which read "Meet us tonight – 9 o'clock – same place". We thought this was so funny we stopped one of our parents' friend who was on her way to the boat to show it to her.

From her reaction she didn't think it was funny and told us not to go. Of course we had no intention of going, we were only twelve and in any case we were not allowed out at that time of night. The neighbor must not have told our parents; otherwise we would have been grounded.

Liberty ships in the harbor

My home was originally Brackett farm land and pastures. I've been told by a former owner that the house is very old, older than the City of Portland records indicate, and was the only house in the area for several years. It used to be referred to as the old Hadlock place and was a dairy farm. There is a story in several Peaks Island history books about a shipwreck on September 8, 1869. The *Helen Eliza* of Gloucester Massachusetts, captained by Edward Millett of Rockport Massachusetts, was shipwrecked during a violent storm and came ashore at night on the rocks on the south-east side of the island. Charles Jordan of Rockport was the only survivor. He saw a light in a window of a farmhouse and was able to reach it. It was the home of Sam Hadlock. The bodies of the rest of the crew and the remains of the ship were later washed ashore on the harbor side of the island.

The island has always attracted those who march to a different drummer. The most colorful were the actors who came each summer in the 30's and 40's to Greenwood Garden Playhouse. They rented cottages or stayed at the Avenue House. They would walk along Island Avenue reciting their lines. Some of them were very friendly while others ignored us completely. We spent a lot of time around the theatre, especially at show times. We took tickets, ushered, helped move sets, did odd jobs, and ran errands. (All this for free seats at the show!)

The Casco Bay boats were steamers and the crew wore uniforms. A few of them have a very special place in our memories. Probably our all time favorite boat was the *Sabino* with Eunice's dad as captain. The upper deck was all open. The lower deck had a small ladies cabin with red velvet cushions. There was a larger cabin beyond with seating for passengers overlooking the engine-room. We used to watch the engineer stoke the furnace. Unlike boats with engines, steamboats were relatively quiet unless one was close to the engine room. Some years an accordion player and his wife entertained us with music, before we landed, his wife would pass the hat around.

Our high school boat was the *Emita*, a much larger boat with ample inside and outside seating on both decks. It had a very large smoke stack going through the upper deck cabin. It was warm to the touch and a favorite spot on cold days for students (which included Cliff and Long islanders). Warren, our purser, was usually sitting in our midst helping one or more of us with our homework. The lower deck was mostly enclosed with seating and also had a large ladies cabin, again with red velvet cushions.

Some of the boats went down the bay stopping at some or all of the landings depending on the schedule. If you weren't paying attention or napping you could easily miss your stop. My mother found herself on the way to Great Diamond Island one time. Fortunately, her friends, the Carrs, brought her back to Peaks in their boat; otherwise she would have to stay on the boat until it returned to Peaks on the way back to Portland.

Saturdays, during the cooler weather, were days to go "uptown". We walked or took the bus to Congress Street where all the action was. There were several theaters, restaurants, drug stores with soda fountains, and five and dime stores along with nice department stores and office buildings. Further up Congress Street was the Portland Public Library. Many Portland residents and islanders worked in the area. There were also several banks, doctors' offices and hospitals.

Buses were constantly coming and going in Monument Square. One of the five and ten cent stores had a lady singing and playing the piano, plugging sheet music. Kids from all over Portland came for a movie, to shop, or to have a soda at H. H. Hays drug store. We never heard the word "Mall" but Congress Street had everything we could ask for.

We had such good times in those days, like playing house under Reta's lilac tree or in her Dad's camper, or swimming off Eunice's grandfather's slippery boat ramp.

We swam at the beaches, went picnicking on the rocks, and jumped or dove off the wharves. Trefethen Landing was a favorite. It extended out several feet from the shore to accommodate the Casco Bay Boats at low tide, but because of the currents it could be dangerous. I found this out the hard way. One day, after jumping in, I swam easily, too easily, towards Evergreen. When I turned to head back, I realized I was swimming against a very strong current. It took a great effort to get back to the wharf. That was the last time I swam off that dock.

We picked berries, rowed to and explored other islands, and sailed on John Brackett's sail boat. I remember winters as being very white with huge snow drifts (great for making snow forts). There were good hills to slide on and several ponds for skating and the older boys used to make ski jumps. After school on those cold wintry days I often went to Reta's house and we listened to our favorite "soaps" on the radio.

1st and 2nd grade. Joyce, 2nd row, 3rd from left and
Reta, 5th from left

It has been so enjoyable putting this collection of memories together with Reta, Eunice, Alice and Ellin. Many years have past since those days, even so, as I walk along the shore and see a perfect tide at Rocky Beach, or see queen Anne's lace blowing in the breeze, or maybe find a lady's slipper while walking in the woods, I feel like a child again.

END OF STORY

WE HAVE ATTEMPTED to "paint a picture" of what life was like with this collection of memories from our childhood. So much has changed yet so much remains the same. It was then, and still is, a most beautiful island.